A TREATISE ON ANCIENT HINDU MUSIC

ARUN BHATTACHARYA

South Asia Books

COLUMBIA, MISSOURI

First Published : 1978

Published in the United States of America by
SOUTH ASIA BOOKS, Box 502, Columbia, Mo. 65201
By arrangement with
K. P. BAGCHI AND COMPANY, 286 B. B. Ganguli Street, Calcutta 700012, India.

Printed in INDIA at Santinath Press, 16 Hemendra Sen Street, Calcutta 700006.

A TREATISE ON ANCIENT HINDU MUSIC

To

Shri Rajyesvar Mitra

my esteemed friend

PREFACE

I have not attempted at writing just a history of ancient Hindu music. More competent persons had done it earlier. Nor have I searched for new materials as historians would like to do. I have drawn material from the standard texts in Sanskrit, Bengali and English languages.

What I have actually tried to discuss within a brief span is to link up the entire history in a systematic manner, avoiding over-lapping of incidents. Secondly, I have attempted at explaining, so far my knowledge permits, some of the debatable passages. Thirdly, there are new interpretations of accepted concepts; therein I have tried to be somewhat original in my thinking. I leave it to my readers either to accept or to reject my interpretations. Lastly, I have taken up only those texts which, while connected together, would form a consistent pattern so that my readers would be able to study the inner link of ancient Hindu music, ranging from the pre-Vedic to the 13th-14th centuries. True, I could not add any new material to my treatise but I have sought to lay down my personal observations, which I think, are quite different versions, though not beyond dispute by scholars in the field.

While foundations of Indian music rest on a definite philosophical bias, the present author has not overlooked the pragmatic as well as realistic basis of raga formation. He has been particularly careful about all probable sociological implications as to the source knowledge thereof. The anatomical description of the human body and of the sound production by Sarangadeva is neither spiritual nor elusive, but rests on purely physiological studies.

I have stressed firstly, on the evolution of raga pattern and secondly, on the aesthetic aspects of Indian music. I have quoted the most relevant Sanskrit slokas and rendered them into roman scripts, and have given explanations thereof for the convenience of non-Indian readers. This book would serve twofold purposes, that of the study of the history of Indian music, as well as of musicology proper.

Criticisms of the musicologists are abundant in this treatise and the present author has been highly critical in his assessments of the major writers and their commentators all through. A comparative estimate of raga names and structures has been brought to facilitate readers for a closer study of ancient and modern practices. Though attempted from a purely academic and artistic plane, this would serve the purpose of a text book at Degree and Post-graduate levels and a ready reference guide for research scholars in the field.

In spite of best attempts there have been a few printing errors. Footnote numbers 3 and 4 should be taken as 4 and 3 respectivcly in p. 8, the word 'suggest' should be read in p. 50, line 25, Bindusara should be read in p. 41, line 7. Discrepancy as to the spelling of Indian names has been settled as far as possible.

Diacritical marks could not be used in the text proper, but the index has been set in diacritical marks. Slokas in roman scripts have been rendered also in diacritical marks along with devnagri scripts. For some proper names, the spelling has been at places devised to suit the phonetic expressions closely. While translations from the Natyasastra and the Sangitratnakara have been done by Manomohan Ghose and C. Kunhan Raja, the present author is responsible for the translation from Naradiyasiksha and Brihaddesi. The Siksha by Narada has been termed Naradisiksha by many commentators. I have preferred spelling it as Naradiyasiksha.

No word is enough to acknowledge my indebtedness to Svami Prajnanananda who has always guided me in all my pursuits in the field. Needless to mention, I have taken ample materials from his standard works. Dr. Niharranjan Ray, who takes a keen interest in all the branches of fine arts, has always inspired me. Prof. D. C. Mitra, Head of the Deptt. of Music,

Rabindra Bharati University, has shown personal interest in my researches. Thanks are also due to the librarian and his colleagues of the Rabindra Bharati University, the Asiatic Society, the National Library and of the Sanskrita Sahitya Parishad. My revered teacher Pandit Sarada Charan Sastri has guided me in interpreting some of the debatable passages of the Sanskrit Texts. I am no less indebted to Shri Ashim K. Ghose, Secretary, State Sangit Natak Akademi, for his constant inspiration, specially for the Kalighat patua drawing that he so kindly lent me from his collection. Shri S. Bagchi did the strenuous job of typing out the MS. Shri Parimal Bagchi and his younger brother Shri Kanak Bagchi have taken great interest in publishing such an intricate and academic treatise. I am specially obliged to all of them.

It is a pleasure for me to dedicate this book to my eteemed friend Shri Rajyesvar Mitra who has devoted his entire life to the study and research of Indian music.

Arun Bhattacharya

September, 1977
Deptt. of Music & Fine Arts
Rabindra Bharati University
CALCUTTA 700 007

CONTENTS

An Apology

The development of Indian music is one of the most fascinating chapters of Indian history. With it are connected not only the various branches of fine arts, but poetics, drama, aesthetics, and last but not the least, some general principles of science, specially acoustics and mathematical equations, which are required to obtain the essential harmony within the melodic pattern of svara structure. Strange though it might seem, the concept of Indian music envisages all these aspects in its totality. Scientific principles are at bottom of svara evocation ; therefore these are not the last observations, but are fundamental in evaluating the unity in theme and design of a raga ; rather, the melody pattern of Indian music. That these melody patterns are categorised within the ten thatas, as in northern Indian music or within the seventy-two melas as in the Carnatik styles, is also a result of systematization that bases itself on a scientific outlook. That the bistara or svara prastara of a raga has its own distinctive sequence is also the result and outcome of the mathematical deduction of the permutation formula $^{n}p_{r}$. Thus the very structure of raga music is based on some scientific, rather mathematical principles that give it a shape and contour ; while its inherent beauty lies in the proper assessment and evocation of the poetics, the dramatic and the aesthetic qualities of human imagination. Under the context it may, therefore, be ascertained that Indian music encompasses such apparently contradictory subjects of knowledge and ultimately verges on philosophic intuitionalism.

The study of history of our music of the past, both ancient and mediaeval, has been discouraged by some eminent musicologists, as Pandit V N. Bhatkhande. He is of the opinion that our past history has no bearing on the modern practice. Music, essentially being a practical study, does not, therefore, depend on the pattern, long dead and gone. But Pandit Bhatkhande has perhaps observed only a partial view of the subject which has so many definite facets.

A proper study of the history of Indian music firstly takes us to a long and distinct tradition. Unless one does not know the tradition of his subject of study it becomes difficult for him to have an objective view. The tradition of Indian music, both classical and romantic, ranges over a period of a few thousand years and that it has been a live subject is the result of its continuity in tradition despite serious and sometimes disastrous political changes in our history. It is commonly known from authoritative books on history that the Mohammedan conquest, overriding this vast sub-continent during the twelfth thirteenth centuries A.D., destroyed not only the Hindu temples, monuments and so on, but manuscripts also to a great extent through succeeding ages. It tried to demolish and subdue the traditional culture ; but the Hindu view of life and its associated culture has had such a deep-rooted tradition, based essentially on a broad philosophic perspective that it has, till now, survived the Mohammedan and Portuguese onslaughts, as well as the so-called British culture cult.

An awareness and pursuit of this tradition can only bring life into the contemporary study of history. It is true that we have long lost our marga geeti, we have now scanty knowledge of the dhruva and the prabandha ganas, so far their practical aspects are concerned; but the study of their nature as well as structural design definitely enriches our mind and leads us to a comparative study of the past music with the contemporary one, resulting thereby a better fruition of our modern patterns.

Along with the tradition a keen student of history becomes aware of the gradual development of music forms, its divisions and branches as well as the culmination of tonal patterns into distinctive individual structures that ultimately came to be known as ragas. The consciousness about this development makes one capable of doing further researches into the probable future of music forms and patterns and helps bring about new discoveries in the field.

A perfect knowledge of the tradition and development of Indian music leads one to an accurate valuation. What Pandit Bhatkhande really did [but decried !] in his well-known treatise on the 'Leading Music Systems of India' was but the result of his persistent study of the tradition and development of the Indian raga music and its formal structure. This has helped Pandit Bhatkhande not only to evaluate our music properly, but has brought about and thrown definite light on the then prevailing music systems. That Pundarika Vitthala of the South wrote in his Ragamala and Ragamanjari about the music of the North, that Rama Amatya, in his Svaramelakalanidhi, traced out the earlier systems faithfully, that the Mankutuhala, edited by Raja Man Singh Tomar of Gwalior, was translated into Persian by Fakirullah during the reign of Aurangjeb [who could not stand music at all !] were significant not only of the records of the valuation of Indian music alone, but are definite documents of Indian history too.

Along with this valuation a scholar might record also the comparative estimate of music types—region-wise, culture-pattern-wise and so on. It is now widely known that India has had one broad music system and grammar ; but along with the Mohammedan conquest the North became separated from the South to a great extent, resulting thereby a distance or culture gap. The North Indian style took its own way assimilating some of the Persian styles ; while the South retained its original integrity. Thus, a comparative estimate became necessary which persists till today. There is also the great factor of raga development and one observes the same comparative structure in a number of modern ragas that had its heritage through the distant past. Malva-Kaisiki, Gurjari, Hindol, Sanjhgiri are such a few names only that need careful scrutiny.

But the student of our music history frofitably gains by this self-exploration in the ultimate analysis, which leads him to formulate a wider perspective of things in general. This generalised view of objectives, gathered from specific roots, genres, styles and idioms are symptomatic of a philosophic view that leads him to the depth of all that are desired in music patterns. Only then a student can really obtain the practical shades arising out of its theoretical context. Music becomes, only then, a live subject that integrates his very being with the broad Nature and its canvas. Raga is not only a system that arises out of mathematical permutations, but an imaginative structure when the musician's passion, zest and love for the essential unities in Nature can best find its expressions. Indian music thereby becomes a 'marga' or a path leading to the highest ideals of man, that is conterminous with his own self-exploration—the realties are not only conceived, but perceived as well in its entire process.

Creative Awakening

All art, even science, rests on creative imagination. Imagination is not divorced from thinking ; and as thinking, in a proper way, leads one to be logical, imagination therefore, has a rational basis in its own way. Music is imagination itself so far the musician tries to explore the interrelation of sound and of musical tones and semitones in order to reflect and communicate his own imaginings to the listener. But in doing so, he has to build up the edifice in a way where method and arrangement are exclusively necessary. In demonstrating a raga, (say, in the dhrupad or khyal form) a musician has to consider a number of aspects which relate either to imagination and feeling on the one hand, and to method and system on the other[1]. It is within this framework that he tries to explore the possible sources of his creation, retaining the basic pattern of that tune and again maintaining, at the same time, the specific form.

'Music and poetry', observed Sourindra Mohan Tagore, 'have been combined from time immemorial. There is a sanskrit stanza to the effect that music and poetry are the two seats of Sarasvati, the Goddess of the two arts. Rhythm connects the musician and the poet into a brotherhood'[2]. Rabindranath Tagore interpreted Music and Poetry as arising out of a common aesthetic bond[3]. Music began to develop more or less as a pattern out of the human speech ; and speech-music, culminating into chants and hymns of the vedic age, found in it, at a later stage, certain decisive forms. Though it is difficult to find out actually what were the existing forms of music at that time, it might be deduced, more or less in a scientific manner, that a system was slowly being developed leading Indian music at that time to some definite pattern. It may be seen from texts that when Samagana was falling out of practice during 600-500 B. C. , 'the laukika gandharva type of systematic-cum-scientific music gaining ascendency over it'[4]. Here we find a positive reference to systematic as well as scientific music. And form, as such, has its significance only when a systematic pattern evolves ; and evolves in a scientific manner. It may be seen, at some later date, to what a great extent scientific observation is essential in the formulation of a raga. In fact, emergence of raga in Indian music is one of the very best examples to show how imagination and intellect could best develop side by side.[5] An etymological definition of music may also be found in Monier-Williams' lexicon.

Indian music was thus bestowed with a form at a period when the musical exponents tried to explore their imaginative heights in a spirit of rationality and judgement. Here was required self-imposed discipline, and was further demanded thorough observation of the simultaneous patterns and groupings. Out of the various patterns arose certain musical types, e.g. , laukika-gandharva type, which may be ascribed with certain definite forms. The earliest form in Indian music is lost to us to-day, but the historical records show that music of India was a very living form transcending various patterns at different stages of its development.

Before Indian music evolved into certain distinct form, the musical pattern was based on one, two or three notes named arcika, gathika or samika respectively. The chantings of Samaveda were recited in the three registers (Sthana svaras) udatta, anudatta, and svarita. The notation of the gayatri mantra *'Om tat sabiturbarenyam'*, etc., uses the R of the middle octave, N of the lower octave and S of the middle octave [The Mode of Singing Sama Gana]. It took a long time to develop the three notes into seven as Madhyama, Gandhara, Rishava, Shadja, Dhaivata, Nishada, Pancama (in the descending order) relating to the later notes prathama, dvitiya, tritiya, caturtha, mandra, atisvarya and krushta. Reference to more minute semitones was given definite connotation as srutis not earlier than the period of Narada and Bharata during the 1st and 2nd centuries A. D. approximately.

Narada had termed these srutis as Dipta, Ayata, Karuna, Mridu and Madhya. When a total of twentytwo srutis evolved at a later date, Bharata arranged them under those original five microtones and named them as Jatis or Adharas. The names of the five Jatis would perhaps reflect an imaginative and symbolical interpretation ; and musicians and musicologists alike were also conscious of the rasa or bhava or the predominant sentiment that music could evoke even at that initial stage of development. [Jati had, of course, another connotation] .

To discuss about the form proper of Indian music, there could be seen two simultaneous developments ; the first centering round the svara staucture that led to the evolution of raga through Jati ragas and Grama ragas ; the second evolving out of the style of singing that led to Geetis to different kinds of Dhruvas, Prabandhas and Rupakas, etc. The evolution of raga, to my mind, is more fundamental, the concept of which is derived out of the creative effort of the musicians, to whom both imagination and intellect were primary essentials.

Looking back at the earliest stage of civilization, or even before that, the nomads and the tribal people had, in their primitive life, some form of music, which may be termed as 'functional'.

Their immediate responses to certain sentiments of sorrow and joy found echo in long wailing or exhilarating sound with just one or two notes. As their group life became systematized and socially organized, they tried to compose harmonic tunes. Such evidence may even be found in the tribal war songs or in merrymakings—accompanied with dances at times, in the Santhal Parganas or Ranchi or interior districts of Madhy Pradesh.

When the Aryan Civilization reached its glory in the vedic period, we find the samana chantings and samana singing as prevalent forms of music. These chantings and singings in the later stage developed itself into four different kinds as gramageyagana, aranyageyagana, uhagana and uhya (rahasya) gana. The singing process of the Samagana was not very simple, its method was quite elaborate consisting of five to seven tones. A more developed form emerged round about the period 600-500 B.C., which was termed as gandharva music, having seven suddha jatis. Some are of the opinion that the jatis were ragas themselves which had the power to create pleasing sensations. During the Buddhist period, music formed a vital part of drama and we know, from the Natyasastra of Bharata, elaborate details about music of the period connected to, and comprising a part of, drama itself. Ragas and geetis had also interchangeable words and usages like jatis, jatiragas, gramaragas ; and geetis had a deep and abiding connection with one other. During the 4th century A. D. or so, jatiragas were taken to be a more definite and systematic form of music. Gramaragas were also mentioned in the texts of the 2nd century A. D.

But these were all preparatory stages in Indian music which actually culminated in a definite form in the Prabandha Geetis and later in the Dhrubapada through a complicated process of creative awakening.

1. "Sangit sastra may be considered in a two-fold view—as a science and as an art"—S. M. Tagore : Six Principal Ragas.
   "Music was, therefore, justly considered by the ancients as the key to all Sciences and Arts, the link between metaphysics and physics through which the universal laws and their multiple applications could be understood : Alain Danielou [Introduction to the Study of Musical Scales].
2. S. M. Tagore : Universal History of Music.
3. Swami Prajnanananda : A History of Indian Music.
4. This aspect has been dealt by the present author in his earlier works
   a. Sangitchinta b Rabindrasangitey Svar Sangati O Surabaichitra c. Dimensions.
5. Sir William Jones : On the Musical Modes of the Hindus [Asiatic Researches].

In Retrospect

It is, however, impossible even to have a fleeting impression of the ancient Indian music in this short, though specific, reference. The first systematic record of this development was laid down in the Naradiyasiksha, considered to be an important treatise of music of this land.

There were, of course, evidences of the development of music of the vedic period in accounts earlier than that of the Naradiyasiksha. At later dates, Acharya Sayana, in his commentary on the Riks, had elaborately dealt with the process of the rituals, songs and dances which formed integral parts. Katyayana refers to the entire process as

Nrityagitavaditrabachha

which signifies that music itself was a composite art. Reference to various veenas as kanda, aghati, satatantri, katyayani was found in the scattered literatures of the period. A bow instrument named pinga, and dundhuvi and benu were also mentioned. Apart from Picchola and oudambari veena, there was also another variety as kshoni, used specially during the chanting of the hymns.

The most important factor seemed to be the variety of ways in which the vedic songs were reproduced :

Samavedey sahasrang gityupayah

In fact, the hymns were composed according to various sakhas and prasakhas and each type had its own tonal characteristics. As many as four to seven notes were used even in that period according to the composition :

etairbhabaistu gayanti sarbah sakhah prithak-prithak

The above rendering from the Samapratisakhya would clearly show that there were ample scope of variation in the actual rendering of the hymns. Even the existence of community or mass singing, as referred to in the word 'ganageeti' (in Puspasutra), cannot be ruled out.

There are also stray references to svaras as hrasva, dirgha and pluta in the Aranyakas and Upanishads. Unless some one had an accurate conception of the time-scheme that was required to recite the hymns, it was almost impossible for him to chant with the desired effect that it demanded.[1] In the Rikpratisakhya these three words were treated as units of time, the pluta being thrice the hrasva, and the dirgha being twice the hrasva in time-unit, and these three was compared to the duration of crying of the birds peacock, crow and nilkantha respectively. This reference could be found in later writings also.

The relation between the seven samik notes and the seven loukika notes, developed later, was first specifically mentioned by Narada in his Sikshas; and consequently, this finding has been an outstanding achievement for this great scholar in evaluating firstly, the transition of the vedic music to the laukika one and secondly, the relative structural pattern of notes of these two kinds of music.

Some of the pratisakhyas and sikshas were more philosophical in their delineation of the term nada and svara and the concept of the physical universe could be found latent therein. It may be pointed out that in later years, Sarangadeva also, in describing the origin of nada, pointed to physiological aspects in his reference of the srutis as

hridyurdhanarisanglagna

This account was again faithfully reproduced by Abul Fazal in his Ain-i-Akbari.

But it is in the Naradiyasiksa that a detailed and systemetic account of the music of ancient period has been faithfully recorded. In trying to make one feel the relative merits or the contribution of Natyasastra, Brihaddesi or the Sangitaratnakara, the exposition of the Naradiyasiksha is, therefore, essential. The music of the ancient period may roughly be divided into four succeeding ages: 1. Vedic period, 2. Post-Vedic as in Sambidhana Brahmana, Sikshas and Pratisakhya, 3. Epics and 4. Puranas. While Naradiyasiksha throws light on the vedic period and tries to connect it with laukika songs, Natyasastra elaborately details out the jati and gramaragas on the one hand and the Dhruva geetis on the other. Matanga's Brihaddesi was written at a time between the emergence of Bharata and of Sarangadeva. Matanga's method is highly philosophical and poetic, while it does not lack system. But it is in the Sangit-Ratnakara that the fullest and the most comprehensive account of the ancient Hindu music is to be found. And it was left to Locana, the court-poet of King Ballal Sena of Bengal, to start afresh with the music of the mediaeval period. It is interesting, however, to learn that Locana was living some hundred years earlier than the author of Sangitratnakara. It is unfortunate that Locana Kavi has not been given his due ; in fact, the mediaeval music history that sharply deviated itself from that of the ancient period, started with Locana's writings. His exposition of the ragas into janaka and janya types is the first scientific attempt at raga classification that culminated in the nineteenth century to thata and raga, popularised by V. N. Bhatkhande [according to a few historians Locana Kavi's date is specified at a much later time, particularly Dr. Sukumar Sen holds this view].

1. Advanced students may kindly refer to Ajodhyanath Sanyal's 'Vaidic Svararahasya'.

Transformations

Stage I : Pre-Vedic Period

The primitive man discovered once that a simple harmonious sound or the blowing of the wind, 'perhaps the twang of his bowstring was a pleasure in itself[1], he could thereby imagine the rudimentary form and beauty of music. His imagination led him to discover new sounds of a pleasure-giving kind and to master the art of blending and weaving these together so as to get the maximum of enjoyment. Music, as a highly developed form of art at a later period of human civilization, became the direct outcome of an aesthetic urge for expression. The vehicle was sound and the communicative impulse arose from a latent urge which may be more precisely termed as aesthetic imagination.

Curt Sachs[2], in his interesting work on the music of the ancient world, presents three traditional theories as to the origin of music from the primitive source. Imitation of animals, as referred to, was associated with the origin of svaras. Indian musicologists held the same view. The seven notes as S R G M etc., are the direct result of imitating the tone and pitch of seven different animals and birds

Sadjey badati mayuro gabho rambhanti carshava
aja badati gandharo crouncanadasna madhyamey
puspasadharaney kaley kokilah pancamey svarey
asvastu dhaivatey praha kunjarastu nishadaban

Almost the same sloka appears in the Siksas. Secondly, music was conceived as a means of facilitating team work. This conclusion led to a more practical view as to the origin of music. Thirdly, that music descended from spoken language and that it was nothing but 'intensified speech[3], has a scientific, specially physiological significance. The sama stotras, i.e., slokas, may be considered as intensified speech at a very early stage of Indian history and the slow rise and fall of the sounds of those slokas aroused in the listener's mind a kind of aesthetic sensation. Those incantations were no music, but had the rudiments of music latent within. Curt Sachs made his own observation when he commented that music began with singing, thereby implying that singing is a process mixed up of words and tunes that led to the higher form of imaginative expression termed as music. In thus viewing music he imparted in it a philosophical context. In singing, therefore, were expressed 'force and specific animation', the words and sounds, and the timbre and pitch which resulted ultimately in the suggestion of melodies. Music was no mere abstract melody pattern in those ancient days, but had a sociological basis as it was a form of prayer, an act of healing, and served sometimes as magic incantation. In folk songs of India as well as of other countries, the words sometimes had lost their meaning ; rather, meaningless nonsense formed the body of music, and regular periodic tempo highlighted the simple tunes. Rudimentary those patterns though might be, the melodies did follow an order and sequence. These were repetitive. Curt Sachs further emphasized that primitive music depended more on routine and instinct ; the instinct, of course, was nothing but a physiological process of imagining, and routine but its order.

As music developed from its primitive form to the days of relative maturity, mere imagination of the primitive man became a cultivated one ; and experience, knowledge and higher aesthetic sense combined to give proper shape and cohesion to the music which was just an impulse with the ancients. The earliest record towards the formation of organised music was set down by H. A. Popley, describing the trend as trying to make 'a bold plunge for the nearest consonant note'.

Imagination, being ultimately responsible for the origin of music,—to be more precise,—the urge for imaginative expression[4], from the aesthetic point of view, had certain constituent elements as its direct and immediate responses. Some historians refer to music as the primitive urge for expressing emotional outbursts ; others point out that musical sound is the natural expression of human feeling,[5] and that the origin of music dates back to the pre-historic times when even language was not born. That human feeling has a direct and immediate bearing on music and further that feeling is but a corollary to the imaginative response of man in general, has been substantially proved at later dates when the rasa theory was expounded by so many aestheticians in the rendering of Indian ragas and raginis. The sentiments evoked were manifold and these were exemplified at great length. Even the individual tones and micro-tones have their specific sentiments, while a raga may evoke unitary or multiple sentiments at the same time. Psychologists have experimented with a variety of musical sounds at different conditions and have tried to prove conclusively that as many as nine varying emotional traits have been found to exist in human nature as a result of hearing good music. Max Schoen, an American scholar, has noticed that music is the immediate cause of change in the existing state of a listener and that this change may be classified broadly in nine categories as dreamy tranquil and soft, sentimental and passionate, sad tragic and mournful, solemn spiritual and grave, cheerful and gay, graceful, spirited and exciting, martial and majestic, sensational and thrilling.[6] These revelations are, of course, no new theory for the Indian scholars. The entire raga music and its bearing on human mind had long been discussed at length corresponding to its emotional impact ; and varying sentiments had been attributed to the specific ragas. However, uniformity of thinking in the eastern as well as western mind proves conclusively that not only music had an imaginative background but also had evocative power and that higher music is the outcome of man's urge for proper and systematic expression of his aesthetic imagination.

Primitive man imagined certain sounds as concordant, certain sounds as happy and exciting ; he further imagined that these sounds thrilled somewhere his own emotive responses.

Consequently, when he felt he should express himself, his earlier imagination led him to express such sounds either quite independently and naturally or by way of imitation. Imitation was also considered as a natural way of expression with mankind and found to be inherent within as a qualitative gesture. Expression and imitation, at a certain period of human progress, were almost identical qualities in man [Plato and Aristotle may be examined in this context].

As human beings organised themselves, a new pattern grew out of the primitive music, which might be termed as folk type. There could be found, even in the folk music, certain common traits and patterns throughout the world. More organised but highly impulsive, the folk types maintained a ruggedness in tune. The variations are sudden and hightened by sharp rise and fall in tone.[7] Their imagination was not yet organised but somewhere found an aesthetic impulse towards attainment of beauty in the artistic structure of naturally occurring sounds.

Whether the conclusion that folk music is directly responsible for the growth of other forms of music could not be definitely ascertained ; yet studying the various raga names, certain bearing of folk type may be attributed to the raga structure and raga system. S. N. Ratanjankar concludes that all music, may it be religious, popular, theatrical or festive, owes its origin to the folklore.[8] The statement is too general but may be taken as having a certain amount of historic truth. The growth of human civilization has been traced down from the primitive to the modern age through a great period of community living when folk art, folk music and other tribal culture developed. But whether folk music is really the forerunner of such highly systematic and developed raga music of India needs still further clarification.

When our ancients imagined, either from awe and wonder or from more deep spiritual realization, the existence af an all-powerful Divinity, they would exclaim in a continuously high-pitched prolonged accentuation. The sound was like aum (a+u+m).[9] This was obviously single-toned and no music could be traced therein.

A systematic study of Indian music may be traced from the vedic period, and this has been made possible by the earnest efforts of a number of historians and musicologists who had spent their life-long researches in this direction. The broad features of our music were scattered in various manuscripts some of which seemed to be lost due to succesive foreign invasions. The period throughout which our music was undergoing transformations stretched over thousands of years and those were pre-vedic and vedic ages. There were definite references of these types of songs in the Aaranyakas, the Upanishads, the Pratisakhyas and the Sikshas, the most important among which is the Naradiyasiksha, dealt with in a separate chapter later. The Ramayana and the Mahabharata contain much music materials for thorough researches. Haribamsa and the Puranas, specially the Vayupurana and the Markandeyapurana, are quite important from the historical point of view for records of our music history.

About the primitive music of India there are mostly speculative writings than scientific observations. Taking into view the way of their community life and culture-traits, most of these historians and anthropologists have put forward the arguments that 1. their songs were rendered along with dances 2. these were sung in a group, what we call chorus today 3. these songs were meant for some definite purpose, suited to occasion and 4. their songs were primarily ritual in nature. There were monotonous renderings of sounds that generally proceeded along a single note touching occasionally higher or lower notes in sequence. The group dance formed the more important feature of this primitive music. In war or in hunting, in magical performance or in some community rites, or during the birth or death of some members of the family the music has had an important place. Even when their festivity centred round agricultural produce a suitable theme of music came to be in vogue. The folk songs of India still retain these types.

The primitive races had also their music instruments, the most common of these being bow-instruments. Swami Prajnanananda is of the opinion that this particular instrument was later converted into such bowing instruments as violin etc. Pipes and whistles were also not unknown. Some of the primitive races were found to move about in areas of the present NEFA, Arakan, Chhotanagpur, parts of Madhya Pradesh even today. Researches were conducted by historians, musicologists and anthropologists of which Britishers also had a pioneering role. Along with Rakhaldas Banerjee, Raibahadur Dikshit, Dr. Bhandarker there were Marshall, Anderson, Smith, Piggot and Verrier Elwin. Their earnest and lifelong efforts have made our attempts smooth.

The most important civilization before the vedic period, traced down after the primitive culture, is now known as the Indus-valley civilization. The significant discoveries of Harappa and Mahenjodaro practically altered the history and culture of India and even musicologists had to admit that the vedic civilization is not the earliest so far musical patterns are concerned. They, of course, maintain that the ancient music of India is the direct offshoot of the vedic music, but then vedic music is not the earliest in India. The date of vedic civilization and its periodicity as inferred by the scholars has varied widely. Some are of the opinion that the 'Rik-samhitas might have received to final shape in about 1,000 B.C. ; some of its contents are much older, and certainly go back to 1,500 B. C'. On the other hand, Marshall and others pointed out that the pre-Vedic Indus-valley civilization existed between 5,000 B. C. to 3,000 B. C. Some historians have again linked up the two civilizations, that of Indus-valley and the Vedic together stating that 'Indo-Aryans were not strangers to Indus-valley' and that 'the Vedic Aryans belonged to the same ethnic-culture group'.

2

Avoiding this controversy one might more or less definitely state that the Indus-valley civilization, discovered with the excavations of Harappa and Mahenjodaro, was an earlier phase in Indian history than the vedic culture ; that again suggests the period of Indus-valley civilization as continuing between 5,000 to 2,000 B. C., after which the vedas were begun to be written. The music materials that were derived from the relics were considered to be of much importance. A distorted flute, dancing women in bronze, some sort of a stringed instrument resembling veena were found. There was another evidence, that of a bridge (on which the strings of an instrument are placed), found from the Lothal excavation. All these might prove that songs, dances and instrumental music were prevalent at those times. The date of the Harappa culture was taken to be beyond the 2,000 B. C. era. The figure of another woman playing on the instrument (lyre or veena ?) with four strings was found from the Rupar excavations, carried near Ambala in the Punjab, the date of which was of comparatively later years.

Raibahadur Dikshit has given a detailed account of these findings : 'Besides dancing, it appears that music was cultivated among the Indus people, and it seems probable that the earliest stringed instruments and drums are to be traced to the Indus civilization. In one of the terracotta figures a kind of drum is to be seen hanging from the neck, and on two seals we find a percussion of the modern mridanga with skins at either end. Some of the pictographs appear to be representations of crude stringed instrument, a prototype of modern veena ; while pair of castanets, like the modern karatala, have also been found.' Another description by a distinguished archaeologist runs thus, 'One seal has presented a dancing scene. One man is beating a drum and others are dancing to the tune'.

The above references prove that there were both dancing and community songs ; instrument playing was also in practice. But we can not infer the type of songs, nor the style of dancing.

Other investigations prove that the civilization was one of high standard so far materialistic culture was concerned. But the details are still wanting to connect the missing links so as to compile accurately the music history of the people.

1. James Jeans : Science and Music.
2. Curt Sachs : The Rise of Music in the Ancient world, East and West
3. Felber, W.
4. Edward Hanslick : The Beautiful in Music.
5. Krishnadhan Banerjee : Gitasutrasar.
6. O. Goswami : The Story of Indian Music.
7. Niharranjan Ray : Bangalir Itihas.
   Asutosh Bhattacharya : Bangiya Lok Sangit Ratnakar.
8. S. N. Ratanjankar : Folk Songs and Music, Text of a Lecture delivered at the Ceylon Branch of the Royal Asiatic Society and published in its Journal vol 11 Pt. 2, 1952.
9. Vaidik Svararahasya.

Transformations

Stage II : Vedic Period

The vedic period ranges from 2,000 B. C. (3,000 B. C. ?) to 600 A. D., a period extending for more than 3,000 years even from a casual estimate. The family tree of the Vedas may be set up in atabular form as under ;

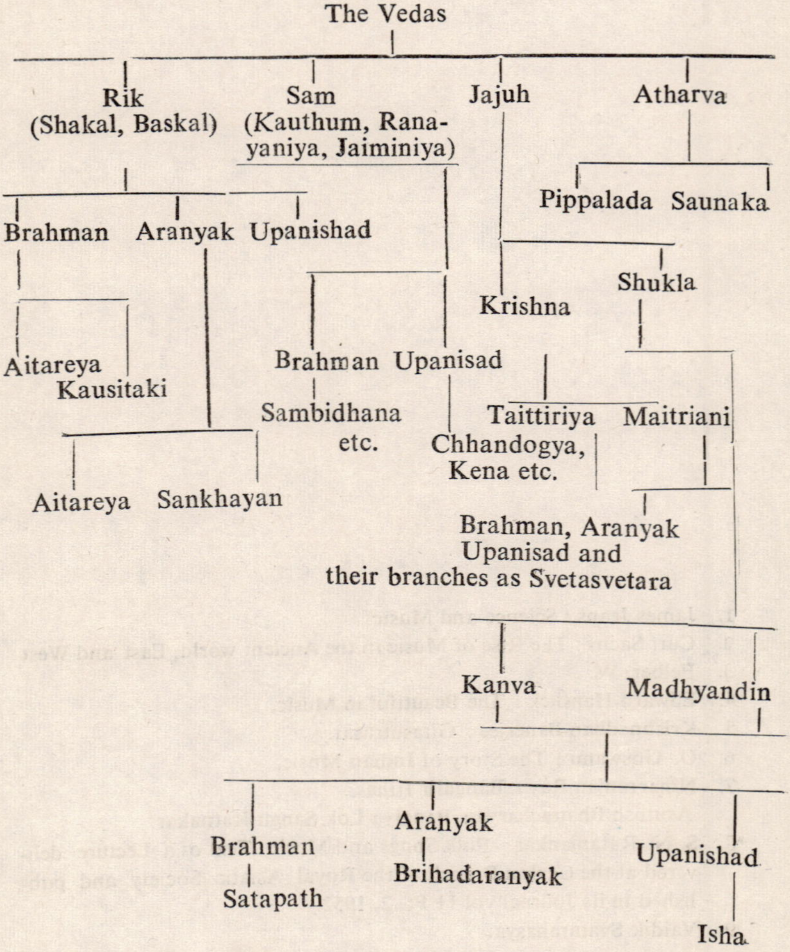

The above table would show to what extent and dimensions the ancient sages (rishis) developed their original thinking and philosophic intuition that were described through slokas, some of which were treated as stotras to be recited in specific tonal accents.[1] This pattern had variations in utterances so far tonal pattern was concerned and ultimately shaped itself to something, that surpassed the stage of recitative function, and encompassed, within its sphere, the rudiments of musical form.

Music in the vedic age is synonymous with the samaganas, though references of music are to be found in most of the broad and lesser writings emanating form all the vedas. At the beginning the samagana, rather a form of chanting, used three notes in connection with the terms as udatta, anudatta and svarita. The first term udatta meant the high-pitched tone anudatta, the low-pitched and svarita, the middle one. In fact, these three terms related to base notes or accent tones that had a relation with the scale of the samagana. Some scholars are of the opinion that these three tones udatta, anudatta and svarita did correspond to the laukik notes rishava (R) nishada (N) and Sadja (S) of frequency proportions 10/9, 8/9 and 1. Even the gayatri sloka '*Om bhurbhoobah svhah*' is recited in fluctuating tones that had its range from R to N in the abaroha krama [descending order]. It may therefore be concluded that these three notes, at an earlier stage, formed, by themselves, a particular scale. At a later sequence gandhara (G) and dhaivata (D) were developed with the frequency proportions as 32/27 and 5/6 relative to Sadja as unit. The scale becomes a complete one when madhyama (M) and lastly pancama (P) came to be introduced with frequency ratios 4/3 and 3/4 respectively. Thus the notes developed in the order SNR/GD/MP which had the descending sequence SNDPMGR. It, however, remains a mystery how the note D came into practice just after the note G, or again, the note M after the note P. The mathematical ratio, taking S as the unit, runs as :

S	R	G	M	P	D	N
1	10/9	32/27	4/3	3/4	5/6	8/9

below or the lower scale

Arranging the sequence in order and converting the figures in the lowest common factor we find [taking S as the unit]

S	R	G	M	P	D	N
108/108 i. e. 1	120/108	128/108	144/108	81/108	90/108	96/108

The ratio shows that the notes R G M are in the ascending order from S, while the notes N D P are in the descending order according to the table of the frequency ratio. The sequence may now be arranged as per frequeny ratio to show the relative svara positions of the major notes as :

P	D	N	S	R	G	M
81/108	90/108	96/108	108/108	120/108	128/108	144/108
Lower octave					Middle octave	
anudatta			*Svarita*		*udatta*	

This sequence shows that the svara-krama was in the descending order as M G R S N D P

which explains two significant points. Firstly, the first note of the sequence was madhyama, secondly the Ma-grama [the word 'grama' meaning at that time the 'scale' i. e. from the Latin word 'scala' corresponding to ladder] was in practice during the vedic period. There is another interesting point and that was related in the Naradiyasiksha that the vedic note S [prathama] corresponded to the laukik note M. But there remains one anomaly still. The descending sequence of the loukik notes was in the order

M G R S D N P

and not in M G R S N D P

According to the laws of acoustics and vibration frequency ratio, this can not be explained, as may be shown in the table just shown above. If the order of the laukik notes are taken for granted, it becomes obvious that the sequence has had not the regularity it should have maintained i. e., it has proceeded along a curved line (bakra gati). Musicologists have widely differed in this aspect. Svami Prajnanananda has given two distinctive views, those of Pandit Ramaswamy and Basudev Sastri on the one hand, maintaining that the bakra gati was in order i. e. D N P is correct ; and of Pandit Lakshman-Sankara on the other, asserting that NDP should be the right order. The views expressed in the Naradiyasiksha of the vakra gati has not been accepted in the Mandukisiksha which quotes the present (accepted) sequence. However, the vedic notes as Prathama, Dviteeya, Triteeya, Caturtha, Mandra, Atisvarya and Krushta corresponding to the laukik notes madhyama, gandhara rishava, sadja, dhaivata, nishada and pancana.

The samaganas were reproduced in six systematic orders termed as 'bikara'. The word bikara suggests the way in which the letters and words, contained in the sloka, were split up in certain specific manner. Whenever there was an interval 'stova' was to be repeated. The stova that was found to be classified in three categories consisted apparently of meaningless words as ou, haou etc. But the beauty of these chantings rested exclusively on the nature and accuracy of pronunciation. It may be recalled here that the pronunciation of the vedic sanskrit slokas are different, to a large extent, from that of the classical sanskrit.

According to the nature of the composition and its ideals the samana songs were broadly divided in four categories as 1. gramageya 2. aranyageya 3. uha 4. and uhya. The number of such songs as available in all the texts run into more than six thousands. The first two types are quite significant from their apparent meaning and suggestiveness, while the last two were not practised in the community as such. These songs had specific purposes relating to 'avicharika' acts, culminating to incidents that are symbolical of healing or destruction as the case might be.

Riks formed the very basis of the samagana. Riks or

slokas (in part or in its entirety) were set to tune and were practised during a sacrifice. The songs were in chorus, someone leading the team and the rest following him. The musician, who led the team, was known as prastota and the sage who initiated the chantings was the ritvika. There were more than one ritvikas depending on the slokas that were taken from the rik, sama, and jajuh vedas having different modes of rendering and accentuation. The introductory or initial song rendered by the udgata was known as stotras or chantings. The chorus team followed later with clappings of their hands, encircling the place of sacrifice.

The instruments that are mentioned in the various branches of the vedas are not insignificant. It was commonly known that the music, from the ritualistic point of view, was divided into two distinct categories as 1. abhyudaiyka and 2. avichaarika. Songs were usually accompanied with instrumental combine and dances, and that is exactly why the sage Katyayana has referred to this fact stated earlier.

1. Research scholars might find an intersting study in the book 'Vaidik Svararahasya' by Pandit Ajodhyanath Sanyal, Burdwan University, referred to earlier.

Transformations

Stage III : Vedic notes and later forms

The type of chantings in vedic songs, extended in a single tone, was called arcika, while two-toned chantings were named gathika. In the next stage, another tone was added and the chantings were mainly uttered in three notes termed as samika with N of the lower octave and S and R of the middle octave. Next came svarantarita with four-toned chants and the accompanying rhythm of the slokas was generally named anustubh. Either D of the lower octave or G of the middle octave was added ; when both these were added at the same time we find, at a later stage of development, the pentatonic scale, capable of producing raga music. 'The Vedic songs, samaganas had their base in a fixed scale which was framed out of five, six or seven vedic tones and these were in a descending series.[1] The seven vedic tones were caturtha, tritiya, dvitiya, prathama, mandra, atisvarya, krushta. These names were obviously different from those of the laukika svaras. But the caturtha note in the vedic scale was concordant and symmetrical with the sadja of the laukika scale and krushta with the pancama. The equivalent notes are as follows :

Vedic notes	*Laukika notes*
prathama	madhyama
dvitiya	gandhara
triteeya	rishbha
caturtha	shadja
mandra	dhaivata
atisvarya	nishada
krushta	pancama

Swami Prajnanananda has quoted from Sikshakar Narada (1st century A.D.) to prove the concordance of the vedic notes with the laukika ones and he further cites Bharata's reference to the laukika seven notes as shadja, rishabha, gandhara, etc,

After these seven notes took shape, the conception of sruti arose and the earliest musicians discovered twenty-two semi-tones as acceptable musical sounds in running order and thus completing a cycle of an octave. The earliest reference to the octave in Indian music found a shape in the form of grama. Reference in the earliest musical texts to three gramas became obsolete even in Bharata's time in the 2nd century A.D., as music in the gandhara grama was said to be practised by the gandharvas for the pleasure of Gods and was beyond the reach of common men. The existence of shadja and madhyama gramas were in vogue round about Bharata's time.

While the seven notes incorporating twenty-two semitones, encompassed within the cycle of octave, and having three successive registers as mandra, madhya and tara, i.e., lower, middle and upper octaves, constitute the tonal structure of music, the geeti varieties were considered as the corresponding form of the same. Different forms of geetis owed their origin to the dramas and as such, Bharata dealt the chapters on music and various geetis within the scheme of Natyasastra. When the curtain was raised after a particular scene, dance and geetis followed along with the instrumental music (Atodhyadi) which described alapa in a particular raga, i.e., jati raga mentioned by Bharata. During the vedic period such laukika geetis were completely absent and in its place only the samaganas formed the only kind of geetis, if they might be so termed. Those were obviously slokas, based on a fixed scale and sung in, even upto, seven vedic tones. The music forms, then derived out of the samana chantings, were broadly four in number as gramageya, aranyageya, uha and uhya [another type as beya gana was also recorded in early literature]. The very names bear relative significance. The Samhitas were divided into three classes as Purvarcika, Aranyaka and Uttararcika. The form, the structure and the method of presentation of these songs, i.e., the four kinds of songs, just referred to, cannot definitely be ascertained now, but depending on the progression and arrangement of svaras and gramas, it might be inferred that the tonal structure of the laukika geetis were but the result of a long and steady process of development of the vedic tunes, though the form and character of the latter geetis differed greatly with those of the former samaganas.

The development of Indian music continued, from the very earliest times, in two parallel and symmetrical lines. The first lies in the progression and structure of notes, their arrangement and order, their balance and harmony, resulting in simple or intricate melody patterns ; the other, in the form and structure of the geetis, their style and technique of presentation. The culmination of the former led to the origin of raga system, while that of the latter, to the establishment of such geeti forms as Dhruva, Prabandha, Rupaka, Dhrupad, Khyal, Tappa, Thumri, etc., Sri Krishnadhan Banerjee was, of course, of the opinion that there were only three major forms of raga music as Dhrupad, Khyal and Tappa ; Thumri, he classified, under Tappa as its offshoot.

Looking back into the complex history of Indian music, it may be inferred that four definite yet different age groups led to such developments from a chronological point of view. Leaving aside the pre-historic times, we can well assume that vedic period bore the first fruits of an organised and systemetic musical culture that was simple yet dignified in character. The early vedic period and its continued chapters as to be found in the Brahmanas, Pratisakhyas and Sikshas might be taken as the formative period of Indian music when we find simple tunes and chantings of mantras. The notes have developed from the arcika to the septatonic, but melody pattern was not constituted. The next period culminated, since then, just before the time of Bharata during the 2nd century A.D., the detailed records of which are to be found in a most authentic manner in the Natyasastra. Simple melodic tunes gave rise to such melody pattern as Jati ragas,—its suddha and vikrta varieties,—the exact word 'raga' is however absent in the Natyasastra ; but the ten lakshmans he refers to Jatis are found to synchronize with similar lakshmanas attributed to the ragas at a later date. We find reference to such music forms, seven in number, named Madrak, Bardhamanaka, Asarita, etc. Seven other suddha geetis as Rik, Panika, Gatha, etc., also existed. The dhruva forms originated as the natural development of geetis, that had direct bearing on the drama proper. Bharata has also referred to Gandharba music as constituting svara, tala, pada, etc., having two forms, nibaddha and anibaddha.

Gandharvang janmayaproktang svaratalapadatmakam
Padam tasya vabedbastu svaratalanubhabakam

Reference to Chachatputah tala and chachaputah talas[2] was to be found thus signifying that the musical forms were gaining a symmetry and cohesion. The third period culminated again during the time of Sarangadeva who, it is said, served as a chief clerk [*Karanagrani*] in the court of one Jadava ruler of Debgiri in the South during the period between 1210 A.D. to 1247 A.D. Sarangadeva referred to the works of Bharata, Matanga, Kohala, etc. He also mentioned names of such grammarians and aestheticians as Lollata and Abhinabagupta. His commentators, both Kallinatha and Simhabhupala, also contributed a great deal in exploring the musical treatise, considered to be the most authentic since the time of Bharata. Sangitaratnakara attains a glory and respect unattained by any other work uptil now. The entire musical system he has described and analysed in details and the manifold and complex structure of musical tunes as well as forms could be ascertained in a very compact yet systematic manner. Descriptions of nada svara sruti, formation of murchhana tan, formation of khandameru, etc., are to be found. Reference to suddha and misra jatis, tala and geeti varieties are there. In the Ragadhaya he has dealt elaborately with the structure and system of ragas, five broad geeti varieties as suddha, bhinna, gaudi, besara and sadharani, names of fifteen grama ragas and their corresponding bhasa bibhasa and antarabhasas, etc.

Such details might easily lead to the belief that during the thirteenth century Indian music culminated to a great height when the raga pattern was firmly established. On the other hand, could be found in the Prabandhadhaya, such intricate and complex references as to the origin of geetis, its subdivisions, formation of prabandha, bastu and rupak, three categories of prabandhas, varieties of suddha and salaga sud, sixteen kinds of dhruva and so on. Rupaka has been defined as a new form quite distinct from prabandha, e. g.,

chhandaganagrahanyasah prabandhabayabairnabaih

trying to explore and combine new patterns. The relative form and structure of prabandha culminating from dhruva as well as that of rupaka might well lead to the belief that the modern form of dhrupada and khyal had their respective origin in these two forms. The last and the modern period, since the time of Sarangadeva has evinced the systematization of ragas into a more methodical way giving rise to mela or thata bibhaga on the one hand, and develoment of such distinct forms of classical music as the dhrupada khyal and their lighter counterparts as tappa thumri, etc., on the other. Instead of jati and gramaragas, and their subdivisions as bhasa, bibhasa and antarabhasas, we now get three broad types of ragas as suddha, salaga and samkirna according to the application of notes, from the structural aspect (in recent times even the difference between the ragas and raginis is not taken into account) and sampurna, shadaba, oudava according to number of notes restricting to 7, 6 and 5.

While the formal structure of classical music rests on such broad divisions as dhrupada and khyal, tappa and thumri, there have been innumerable kinds of geetis with shades of raga tunes as bhajan, dhun, chaiti, kajri, dadra etc., where regional and folk tunes have come into pleasant admixture.[8]

There are certain other forms based on pure tunes, but cannot be termed as geetis, as these are composed with meaningless sounds, principal emphasis being stressed on the rhythmic pattern and tana variations. Such items are tarana, tribat, chaturanga, etc. Instead of conveying pleasant emotional attributes, these types reflect a kind of structural tonal acrobatics having specific slow and fast tempo. These are never demonstrated as principal pieces but sung at the conclusion of a musical performance after dhrupada khyal and thumri. Alapa, in a particular raga, used to be sung at the beginning, succeeded by dhamar and dhrupad, while lighter forms conclude the sequence.

1. Swami Prajnanananda : A History of Indian Music.
2. Chachatputah tala 1st, 2nd & 4th matras guru (2 units each) 3rd laghu (1 unit) chachaputah tala 1st 4th guru ; 2nd 3rd laghu ; pluta is of 3 units.
3. Songs of Rabindranath Tagore, of Atulprasad, Rajanikanta Sen, D. L. Roy are primarily lyrical, but the composers have freely used raga motifs taking into consideration the principal emotive design of the raga as best suited to the ideational process of the lyrics.

Post-vedic Texts

The post-vedic texts are generally commentaries, grammars and other expositions of the vedas and are considered as supplementary additions to the four principal vedas. Reference to Sambidhanabrahmana has already been made where we have found a good number of music materials for our study of the history of that period preceeding the same. The Aranyakas, the Upanishads, The Pratisakhyas and the Sikshas form the most important texts.

The Chhandogya, Brihadaranyaka and the Taittiriya upanishads are responsible for certain fundamental conceptsinherent in music. The utterance of 'om' or 'aum' was to be delivered in a high-pitched tone and so the primary song was termed as 'udgeetha'. This particular word is symbolical of the three aspects of life (prana), utterance (bak) and food, and these again correspond to aditya, vayu aud agni. The actual method of singing the chants were described in details metioning the exact spaces where the hrasva, dirgha and pluta accents are to be introduced. Reference to dancing was also there. The udgana was accompanied with seven other associate notes as binardi, anirukta, nirukta, mridu, slakshna, krauncha and apaddhantva. These were not actual notes, but are the qualitative gestures of the principal svaras as regards their usage. For example, nirukta means clear tone, mridu means softer tones and so on. In the Taittiriyapratisakhya, however, reference to seven sounds are given as upangshu, dhvani, nimad, upabidmad, mandra, madhyama and tara corresponding to inaudible, murmur, whisper, mumbling, soft, middle and loud.

Brihadaranyak is more philosophical in approach and tries to expose the inherent meaning prana, vayu, svara etc. Herein was clearly stated the word 'svaravijnana', which contemplates the art of music as a fundamental science and observes further that the udgata, the principal singer, should have a basic knowledge of the science of svara.

The Pratisakhyas are considered as grammatical texts and analyses and are of the nature of commentaries rather than original treatises. Saunaka happened to be the principal author of the Pratisakhyas. Some are of the opinion that the Sikshas are more important than the Pratisakhyas as the former text covers a wider range. Two very important points are discussed therein. Firstly, the nature of singing the samaganas, the accents on individual letters, the incantation of the words, the rhythmic variations and so on, the repetitive sequence and the admixture of svaras with its corresponding tonal pattern—all these are described. Secondly, as Dr. Winternitz observes, 'The oldest notation is probably that by means of syllables...more frequent, however, is the designation of the seven notes by means of figures 1, 2, 3, 4, 5, 6, and 7 with which F, E, D, C, B, A and G of our scale correspond' [our scale meaning the Western scale]. The notation with numerical digits was in vogue in ancient Hindu music as indicated also by Anne C. Wilson in the treatise on the subject.

The concept of udatta, anudatta and svarita is also discussed. It was stated that udatta is high-pitched, anudatta low-pitched and svarita, the middle. It has again been observed that N and G have been derived from udatta, R and D from anudatta and S, M and P from the svarita. There are names of the seven svaras arcika, gathika, samika, svarantarita, oudava, shadava and sampurna corresponding to the first to the seventh note [these are referred to in all the standard texts. But no reasonable explanation may be found as to the particular classified association of the notes with the udatta, anudata and svarita, regarding their respective groupings]

The present author has found a reasonable explanation considering the relative svara-kramas. Udatta means high-pitched, both the notes N and G are higher than D and R respectively. So the notes D and R are anudatta in relation to the udatta notes N and G. Moreover, it is also interesting to find that N and G arising out of the udatta have the vadi-samvadi relation resting on twelve srutis apart, while D and R, arising out of the anudatta, maintain the same vadi-samvadi relation i.e. these groupings are in perfect harmonic relation.

The word svarita in this context means a balancing or 'link' point wherefrom the principal notes S, M and P have arisen. These three notes, for all practical purposes, balance the the notes N and G on the one hand and D and R on the other. Furthermore, S, M and P are in perfect harmonic relationship, M and P being the samvadi svaras to the basic note S ; these are eight and twelve srutis apart from the sadja note. This explanation, given above, might give us a clue for the classification of the notes as under the udatta, anudatta and svarita. The root meaning of the word svarita has been given in the sanskrit texts as equivalent to *samahara*, meaning compounded of the udatta and anudatta. But how the udatta and anudatta svaras have been compounded remains a mystery as yet.

The significance of hrasva, dirgha and pluta were given earlier. If the hrasva is taken to be the unit of a matra, dirgha is composed of two and pluta of three units of matra. But another practical aspect has also been determined by Saunaka. He has emphasized that the time taken by the bird nilakantha for its utterance of one-syllabic note is to be considered as the unit of a matra, that of the crow, two units and of the peacock, three units of the matra. Moreover, the broad variations of chhanda (rhythmic patterns) were discussed in a specific chapter that begins with the enumeration of different rhythmic sequence. The seven varieties of chhanda that were in use at the time of veda ganas were gayatri, ushnik, anushtup, brihati, pangkti, tristup and jagati.

Pushpasutra happens to be a very important treatise amongst

the Pratisakhyas, that deal mostly with the vedic songs. In fact, this is also termed as an anthology of such songs and interpretations of the mantras. M. Hiriyana has also described the mantras as early specimens of vedic songs in his important work on Indian philosophical systems. The author of Pushpasutra has referred to a type of ganagiti (perhaps meaning chorus !). Stova was performed during the gramageya as well as aranyageya songs.

The Sikshas are quite a few in number as those of Panini, Jajnyabalka, Manduki, Narada etc. Naradiyasiksha, being the most important of all these treatises, has been dealt with in a separate chapter. The sikshas have undertaken the primary task of enumerating the principal points in describing and analysing the music of the time. Panini has given precisely the nature of the exposition of the nada from which, it appears, Sarangadeva has quoted, though, of course, in a different manner. The most important aspect of Panini's work is the enumeration of the concept of sthanasvara for udatta, anudatta and svarita. He has also mentioned eight different positions of human body through which sound comes out and becomes audible to human ear. The svara and vyanjana varnas were correspondingly divided. This approach seems to be quite scientific from the physiological aspect.

Jajnyabalka has not stated anything new, rather repeated traditional concepts though it was accepted that he had a thorough grounding in *saubara* sastra (svarasastra). He has also referred to the three vedic svaras and has accredited these svaras with their relative positions, varna, jati, chhanda etc. The udatta, anudatta and svarita svaras are connected to the gayatri, traistuv (tristup) and jagati chhandas respectively. While these three svaras are referred to as vedic, he has described the notes as sadja etc., related to the gandharva veda. Jajnyabalka has also discussed the hrasva, dirgha and pluta as corresponding to the unit, twice and thrice the time measure, while to vyanjanavarna he ascribed half the matra. But what is more important in his text was the aesthetic view that he tried to impart within the music proper. He has pleaded for sweet, gentle and pleasing music and advised the musician to observe a number of restrictions so as to be able to reproduce good music.

Mandukisiksha is primarily concerned with the Atharbaveda and hence it has very little to do with music proper. Even then the author has touched the salient points as seven svaras, four sthanasvaras as udatta, anudatta, svarita and pracaya (herein do we find his originality to an extent), he has also ascribed to these svàras certain specific :varnas, sthanas etc. It is, however, strange that he has referred to the krushta while describing the laukik svaras (krushta being the vedic note equivalent to the laukik pancama).

The Epics and Haribamsa

The Ramayana and the Mahabharata form the most popular epics of this land and a closer study of these remarkable poetic pieces unravels not only the socio-cultural background of India of the time, but supply us with abundant music materials. It is generally agreed upon that the Ramayana is the earlier text and it is also known that the Ramayana-geeti was sung by Lava and Kusa, two sons of the king Ramachandra. The boys went from place to place singing the sad and tearful story of Ramachandra and his wife Sita. But the fact that the vedic songs were in use at that time is a matter of conjecture, though one might find reference to the samagas in the text proper. Sacrificial rites were not unknown, specially when we note that Ramachandra himself arranged for the Asvamedha jajna. In that particular sacrifice eminent musicians and dancers of the time were invited to participate and Lava and Kusa were asked to sing the Ramayana-geeti.

Gandharva-geeti was in practice at that time, it was noted and later definition of gandharva geeti by Bharata substantiate the fact. Reference to seven suddha jatis as well as of kaisika (kaisika gramaraga !) are there and the words nritya, geeta and vadya frequently occur. The poet Valmiki has given the following description :

Jativhih saptavhirjuktam tantrilayasamanvitam
rasaih sringarakarunahasyaraudrabhayanakaih
biradibhi rasairjuktang kavyametadgayatam

Further, the poet has emphasized that the svaras contained in the slokas of the Ramayana should be of pleasing sound (madhuram). Reference to the various rasas as well as to laya variations incorporating druta, madhya and vilambita are also significant. But there is no reference to the gandhara grama, though Mallinath, the commentator of Mahakavi Kalidasa, refers to gandhara grama at a much later date. The musicians Lava and Kusa were experts in the gandharva-geeti and as gandharvas used to sing in the gandhara grama, one might assume that Lava and Kusa knew the specific style of singing in the gandhara grama. The sage Valmiki is stated to have ordered Lava and Kusa to sing twenty sargas (chapters !) per day

dibasey bingsati sarga geya...

and again

gayatang madhurang geyang tantrilayasamanvitam

A subtle reference to *kaku* also points to the intricate pattern of application of the notes (svara-prayoga) at that time [kaku has been defined elaborately by Sarangadeva in his well-known work].

The aesthetic qualities of the musician were never overlooked. The word 'madhuram' meaning sweet and pleasing, occur in the epic a number of times. The musicians should also be well-dressed and have a good appearance. Reference to percussion as well as stringed instruments as *'atodya'* and *'tantree'* also proves the use of accompanying bands. Vipanci is specifically mentioned,—a variety of veena with nine strings :

Vipanci nabatantrika

Moreover, the citation of venu, sankha, turyya, mridanga, dunduvi, muraja, tala (karatala), ghanta etc. are there. Incidentally, it may be mentioned that some of these instruments were mainly deployed for war purposes and the Mahabharata also cites some of these instruments during the Kuru-Pandava war at Kurukshetra [as described by Sanjaya to Dhritarashtra in the Vismaparva].

Music materials as found in the Mahabharata is scanty in comparison with those in the Ramayana, but the author Vyasdeva has given a philosophic-cum-scientific explanation of the causation of sound, which seems to be of fundamental importance :

ebang bahubidho jneyah sabda akasasambhavah

Akasa [the sky or, astronomically, the celestial sphere] is

the container of all sound. • This realization helps us a lot in understanding the scientific as well as the philosophical aspect of *nada*, the immediate cause of all music. Next in importance is the poet's reference to all the seven notes as sadja, rishabha etc. Therefore, it may be ascertained that these notes, laukik in character, gradually evolved into a distinct kind of music that is neither gandharva nor vedic in nature. Rather, it may be assumed that the deshi geeti, as against the gandharva or marga geeti, began to be evolved at that time, though the poet himself has referred to the word 'gandharva geeti'. In fact, the word 'gandharva' geeti is a generalized term meaning songs of a definite character. • Sacrificial rites were also much in practice and reference to the samagas was to be found at places. But that does not mean that vedic songs were the order of the day, though allusion to the rik and stoma are there in the Santiparva. It may, however, be concluded that the reference to samagas might well prove its prevalence only during the sacrificial rites, and that kings and chieftains did arrange for these sama chantings more as a part of classical or ritual tradition rather than anything else.

Particular reference to mangalageeti in this epic again proves that the character and style of songs have developed from those of the period of the Ramayana. Mangalageeti, as defined later by Sarangadeva, is a variety of the prabandha type which had its existence upto the fourteenth century. Of course, the word 'mangala' may be taken in its general and connotative sense, meaning good or well-being of someone that is derived after such songs are rendered to please the particular deity.

The stringed and percussion instruments of the time include various types of sankha, elaborately described by Sanjaya just before the commencement of the war, saptatantri veena, venu, mridanga, anaka, gomukha, panava, bheri, pushkara, ballaki, devadunduvi etc. The word *baditra* generally means and includes four kinds of instruments as tata, sushira, anaddha (abanaddha) and ghana and all these were referred to in the Mahabharata. While the Ramayana refers to vipanci veena, the latter epic refers to saptatantri veena. Dance is frequently mentioned, but in a casual way. That female dancers had a prestigious place in the society is recorded in the Haribamsa—another epic that remains connected to the Mahabharata as its supplimentary chapters.

Haribamsa introduces a number of sporting festivities ; not only dancing, but songs too, in all its aspects. In the rasa-krira and chhalikya-krira ample references to dancing may be found. In fact, chhalikya has been described as a distinct type of dancing ; womenfolk get a leading part there. The songs introduced within the chhalikya dance were very popular at that time and the Jadava tribes held it in high esteem. Some musicologists are of the opinion that chhalikya gana had been a part of gandharva geeti, because both these terms appear in the Haribamsa in the same sloka.

Referring to the six grama ragas described in the Haribamsa, its commentator points out that these were nothing but madhya, suddha, vinna, gouri, misra, geetarupa and these were sung in the form of ragamala [series or chain of ragas sung in a concert as a single item]. It may be presumed that these six gramaragas referred to in the Haribamsa were later developed into the gramaragas described in the Naradiya-siksha as shadava, pancama, madhyamagrama, sadjagrama, sadharita and kaisika-madhyama or kaisika. But the names in the Haribamsa closely resembles the five geetis prevalent in ancient music as suddha, vinna, gouri, besara, sadharani. As a consequence, it is doubtful whether the gramaragas as described in the Haribamsa actually retained the character of a raga, or those were earlier specimens of geetarupas mentioned as the sixth gramaraga in the series.

There is a detailed account of asarita, taken by the commentator as a form of dancing within the dramatic element. This dance form used to take place after the kutapa-binyasa, a detailed account of which has been given by Bharata Muni in his Natyasastra. The music that accompanied the dance was also termed as asarita, which had three different varieties. There is, moreover, a reference to 'debagandhar' which might be taken as the particular raga known at a later period [or a substitute of the jatiraga 'gandhari' ?]. The significant aspect that immediately attracts the notice of a musicologist is the acceptance of the gandhar grama at that period. The sruti division of the gandhar grama runs as follows :

S	R	G	M	P	D	N
3	2	4	3	3	3	4

though latter musicologists mention the Ga-grama as obsolete.

Some of the percussion instruments used were mridanga, ballaki, turyya, veri, sankha, benu, panaba, dimdim, whereas the stringed instruments that were in use are mentioned as mahati and tumbi [tumburu veena, later transformed into the present tanpura !].

Musicologists before and after Bharata

Before we discuss the relative contributions of the eminent musicologists before and after Bharata, a reference to the Maurya, Bauddha and Gupta era and their cultural attainments would help in a judicious assessment of the music of that period. The Maurya culture had its origin in Chandragupta Maurya and reached its pinnacle of glory at the time of Priyadarshi Ashoka, the son of Bimbisara. The patron ge of Ashoka to Maurya and Bauddha culture was of immense significance—the result of which lasted through centuries. It is also known that Samudragupta had been a great patron of music and that a coin reveals Samudragupta playing on the veena.

Music materials of the time are derived generally from 1. Thera and Theri gathas 2. Kamasutra of Vatsayana 3. Bauddha Jatakas. The Thera and Theri gathas contain nearly one hundred and eighty poems, lyrical in character which, it is presumed by scholars, were sung in accompaniment with instruments at times [Thera and Theris were Bauddha vikshus and vikshunis]. There is a commentary, written about the 5th century A. D. by Dharmapala, which gives us a more or less detailed account of these lyrics. Vatsayana, in his monumental work the Kamasutra, has recorded ample evidences of instrument playing, dancing as well as singing that were elaborately practised during his time. Dramaturgy also found a very important place in his writings ; he has used the word 'prekshanaka' in place of acting. The author has mentioned of sixtyfour kinds of finer arts amongst which songs, instrument playing, drama, dancing, painting have found a very important place. Not only the virgins but the married ladies did also participate in music and dancing. Vatsayana has also referred to deshabhasajnana and chhandojnana amongst the arts, which reflects to what extent the finer arts developed during his time.

A great number of Jatakas refer to various forms of music—the approximate number of such Jatakas, according to historians, vary from 500 to 550 in number. The two Jatakas that are named Nrityajataka and Veribadakajataka obviously contain enough materials for a closer study of the music of the time. A story incorporated herein symbolizes the fact that rhythm or laya is the most vital part of a dance [The peacock could not get the marriage-garland from the lover because it had not the proper sense of laya]. Another such text is Matsyajataka where a reference to megha-geeti is found. This might be the raga Megh developed at a later date. But the story suggests that the singing of megha-geeti brought rains on the earth. There are descriptions also of the saptatantri veena and mahaveena in some of the Jatakas. Lalitabistara, which describes the birth and life history of Lord Buddha, refers to gatha, gana, instruments, dancing as well as

Sankhabherimridangapanavatunavaveenaballaki
.... *snighdhamadhuramanojna*
svaravenuninaditanirghosarutena bodhisattvam...

Lankabatarasutra refers to Ravana's playing on the veena before Lord Buddha in the musical notes

saharsya-rishava-gandhara-dhaivata-nishada-madhyama kaisikī

It is interesting to note that the note pancama is absent and the basic note sadja has been termed as saharsya ; but the way the notes are arranged suggests almost the entire scale. A reference to the existence of a music college at Varanasi is also to be found in a recent historical treatise by Radhakumud Mukherji.

Bharata, in his famous treatise Natyasastra, has referred to Brahma, Narada, Svati, Kohala, Sandilya ; while Matanga, in his Brihaddesi, has mentioned of Visvabasu, Sardula, Dattila, Jashtika, Nandikesvara and so on. If the time of Bharata Muni, the author of Natyasastra, be taken as the 2nd century A. D. and that of Matanga as the 5th century A. D. [most of the musicologists stick to these dates], then it may reasonably be assumed that these musicologists existed during the beginning of the Christian era right almost upto the 5th century A. D.

The minimum details that we can gather about Svati are recorded in Bharata's Natyasastra. Svati's name is associated with the invention of the pushkaravadya, the sound of which resembled that of the incessent overflowing of rains on a tank. Some musicologists also describe him as the inventor of panava and muraja that were used in those days.

The name of Kohala has been referred to not only by Bharata, but also by other musicologists as Dattila, Matanga and Sarangadeva. An earlier text on music named as Sangitameru was supposed to have been written by Kohala and he was respected as an acharya. This work describes both music and dramaturgy and it was pointed out that he wrote also a separate treatise on tala named Talalakshanam. His approach to music was never technical, rather the insight of an aesthetician could be found in all his writings. He has dissected the word 'tala' as an admixture of the spirit of Sankara and Sakti i.e. Hara-Parvati. Kohala has also discussed the cause of dhvani and svara and referred as well to murchhana, which should be used judiciously to expose properly the jatiragas, gramaragas and bhasaragas.

Besides Kohala, historians also refer to the names of Sandilya, Visvakhila, Visvabasu and Sardula, amongst which Visvabasu's contribution seems to be of much importance. In defining sruti, Visvabasu has taken great care and categorically stated that the sound that is distinctly and separately audible is the sruti. About Sardula's contribution to musicology we have to depend much on Matanga who have quoted extensively from Sardula in his Brihaddesi. Sardula has categorised sruti in five standard divisions as dipta, ayata etc.

Of the other few musicologists, Dattila and Nandikesvara deserve special mention though Durgasakti, Jashtika and

Tumburu had also their respective places in the history of Indian music. The work that is generally ascribed to Dattila is known as Dattilam. Dattila has described those songs that were connected to drama and has termed the qualities of the gandharvageeti as *abadhan.* He has mentioned two gramas only, the sadja and the madhyama gramas. About sruti and svara he has coined a new word termed as 'svaramandala'. The nature of svaras as suddha and vikrita is dependent on the varying application of the srutis. The standard suddha and vikrita jatis are eighteen which is the generally accepted number.

Among those after Bharata and before the advent of Matanga, Nandikesvara is considered as the most important musicologist. Some of the definite conclusions that Matanga has expressed in his work are derived mostly from Kohala and Nandikesvara. According to Nandikesvara, not only seven suddha svaras, but a total of twelve svaras are responsible for the murchhanas. He was also acquainted with the jatiragas, gramaragas and bhasaragas ; both the gandharva and deshi songs are mentioned in his work. There are two different manuscripts, generally ascribed to Nandikesvara as 'Nandibharatam' and 'Bharatarthachandrika'. The latter manuscript is supposed by some historians as a summary of the greater work 'Bharatarnaba'. There is also another text named as 'Talalakshmanam', which has directly referred to Nandikesvara.

There are ample controversy as to the date when actually Nandikesvara lived and wrote his works. Saradatanay has mentioned in his work Bhabaprakash that Nandikesvara taught Bharata the art of dramaturgy. Vatsayana has also referred to him as the attendant to the Lord Sankara or Mahadeva. However, the opinion expressed by Nandikesvara is quite impressive and rational in approach. He has unequivocally stated the forms of natya, nritta and nritya and has clearly differentiated the subtle deviation of nritya from nritta, the latter being just the technical know-how of the art, whereas nritya incorporates the artistic and emotive designs and is capable of evocating rasa (lasya). These musicologists including Matanga and Sarangadeva [along with the poet Kalidasa] are responsible for the unfoldment of our musical heritage developed during the post-vedic period down to the 13th century.

Mahakavi Kalidasa is not a musicologist in any sense but music materials are scattered throughout his dramas as well as in the lyrics that speak of his fundamental knowledge about the music of his time. Meghdoot, one of the finest lyrics ever written in any language, records Kalidasa's fine musical sense. Not only has he mentioned the gandhar grama but records also its inherent murchhanas. The famous sloka in the Uttaramegha describes the wife of Jaksha playing on the veena. She was trying to explore the *avicarika* in the gandhar grama so that she could be able to unite with her husband, but her tears, in the mean time, trickled down her cheeks on the strings of the veena. Consequently, the strings could not produce the desired murchhanas [the murchhanas in the gandhar grama are Nanda, Bishakha, Sumukhi, Citra, Citrabati, Sukha, Alapa] for the right and appropriate effect. Actually she forgot, during intense sufferings caused due to separation from her lover, the technicalities of producing the exact murchhanas in the gandhar grama that would help her effectuate the avicarika :

tantriradra nayanasalilaih saraitva kathangchit
bhuoh bhuah svayamadhikritang murchhanang bismaranti

In the same sloka the poet has mentioned of the veena as well as the word 'geyam'. Swami Prajnanananda feels that by the word 'geyam' Kalidasa wanted to mean the prabandha gana, because Mallinatha, Kalidasa's commentator, has explained the sloka in that way.

In the Kumarsambhavam the poet has also used the words murchhana, kaisik and mangalageeti :

murchhanaparigrihitakaisikaih
kinnarairushashi geetamangalah

If the word 'geyam' stands for mangalageeti we may, however, infer to a great extent that Kalidasa had a thorough knowledge of the music-forms and their structure. When we come about discussing Vikramobarsi we find specially the references to various music-forms and dances as charchari, jambhalika dvipadika etc. These were various sub-divisions of *biprakirna*, which arises out of the main stem prabandhageeti. There is also a reference to kukuva. It is not mentioned whether this is the raga kukuva, but the dramatist narrates that it has six 'upabhangas', meaning thereby branches, arising out of it. Various types of dancing are also to be found and the particular mention of *caturasra* definitely proves his knowledge about dance and its various rhythmic patterns. *Caturasra* has elaborately been discussed by Bharata as one of the two main divisions of the prevailing chhanda. Veena (Ballaki), venu etc. are also referred to. He particularly mentions the importance of its technical know-how :

prayoganipunaih prajoktribhih

That Kalidasa had sufficient interest and knowledge about the art of dancing is evident also from Malavikagnimitram. The description of the dancers, their movements with corresponding music and the detailed live sketches of the dancers' figures, appropriate for such an art, are textually narrated.

The greatest among his dramas is Abhijnanasakuntalam which suggests, at the very beginning, the relation of music to seasons. In reply to a question from the actress (the dancer) the sutradhar replied, 'do start your music that suits the summer'. Moreover, the word 'raga' frequently occurs in the text. All these are, no doubt, abundant music materials in the works of the great poet for an assessment of the historical development of our music.

Equally important is the great Tamil work Silappadikaram which gives a fair idea of the South Indian music during the first few centuries of the Christian era. The most important note of the book is its methodical division of the musical scale into twelve equal parts wherein the svarasthanas are placed, dividing the scale into two equal proportions S to M and P to S (of the upper octave). These divisions are called *rashis.* The suddha melakarta raga was Harikambhoji ; sruti was termed *alku* and distinct reference to *alapti* was there. Moreover, the author has emphasized the S-M and S-P relations as the most harmonic and is based on purely scientific considerations.

The Puranas

The very name 'purana' suggests its antiquity and it still remains a problem with the historians to fix up the exact dates of the eighteen puranas that are popularly known even today. The Brahmapurana, Padmapurana, Agnipurana, Matsyapurana, Vishnupurana, Brahmabaibartapurana, Saivapurana, Skandapurana, Markandeyapurana and Vayupurana are the more well-known among the eighteen. Out of these again the last two puranas are important for our study under the context.

By the definition of a purana one understands its five lakshmanas (specific characters) as svarga, pratisvarga, bamsa, manvantar, and bangsanucarita. The fact whether some of the puranas are later additions to the Vedas or written or compiled from time to time as original works is yet to be decided. But this may definitely be ascertained that some of the puranas give us a rough idea about the music of the period ; specially the Markandeyapurana and the Vayupurana state many important items unequivocally which form a definite source for compilation of music materials to connect such a prolonged history.

According to indologists, Markandeyapurana seems to be 'one of the oldest and most important'. Narada, considered to be the main propagator of ancient music, is a very familiar figure with the readers of these puranas and his reference is to be found in almost all the texts. Narada is stated to have asked the apsaras [beautiful women dancers who demonstrated to please the Gods and Rishis only] in the very first chapter of the Markandeyapurana, 'Only those women who have beautiful figures, balanced and evocative of lasya, who are broad-minded and possess genuine qualities, may participate in dancing before me'. According to Narada, it seems, the women who are devoid of such qualities (gunarupabihinaya), are incapable of dancing or they should not be permitted to sing before the distinguished audience.

The puranas are generally written and compiled in a story form. Nagraj (the Lord of the serpants) Asvatara started worshipping the Goddess of Learning Sarasvati. The Goddess became ultimately pleased with him for his devotion and asked him whether he wanted anything for the fulfilment of his ambition. Asvatara wanted that the Goddess should bless his brother Kambal first in a way so that he would be able to assist Asvatara. Next he wanted that the Goddess should give both of them all the knowledge about sangeeta sastra. The Goddess Sarasvati became very much pleased with Asvatara's largeness of heart and gave him the blessings, uttering the words 'both of you would now become conversant with the seven notes, seven grama ragas, seven geetis, seven murchhanas, fortynine tanas and the three gramas as sadja etc.' Moreover, Her blessings included their acquiring the knowledge about padas, talas layas, jatis, todayam (atodyam ?) etc. All the necessary requisites that constitute music proper were bestowed upon the two brothers by the Goddess of Learning. The word 'pada' may mean the lyric, or the music-form or may denote the broad divisions of geeti as anibaddha, nibaddha, anirjukta and nirjukta. The three kinds of layas are quite well-known as druta, madhhya and vilambit, but the three jatis had retained the original sanskritik names as sama, srotogata and gopuchha which have now become part of legend. The two brothers became thus proficient in music (gandharva vidya).

In the various other chapters the names of the musical instruments of many sorts were mentioned, important amongst which were veena, benu, puskara, mridanga, anaka etc. It seems, of course, strange that the author (compiler ?) of Markandeya-purana states of one thousand kinds of veena and benu ! However, this superlative assumption perhaps reveal the expanse and horizon that the music of his time was extended upto.

There is special reference to dancing and the author has

mentioned the names of a few such experts who are traditionally known as Tilottama, Urbasi, Ghritachi, etc. The gandharvas used to sing and these apsaras used to dance and all their manifestations were marked with grace and beauty. Musicians and dancers of the time had a high social status and they were employed in all religious and social functions including those convened at the royal court.

Vayupurana, which is sometimes termed as the Siva-purana or a part of the Brahmandapurana, contains a few important statements apart from describing the common elements of ancient Hindu music. Firstly, the author has no hesitation in referring to music as gandharva, which might conclude that gandharva gana existed during the time. Secondly, the sage's description of the songs reached a high level of philosophic sublimation. The sage was stated to have asked, 'What is that particular kind of music which made the king Raibata feel the eternal time as a second (muhurta or nimesha) only ?' :

Jachhrutva Raibatah kalan muhurtamiba manyatey

Thirdly, the author defined exactly the word 'svaramandal' as comprising of seven notes, three gramas, twentyone murchhanas, and fortynine tanas. Next, the names of the murchhanas, in the gandhar grama guggest their association with the vedic nomenclature as agnistomik, baj-peyik, asvamedhik, rajsuya etc. The fifth assertion of the author of Vayupurana is the existence of three hundred alam-kars (whereas Sarangadeva narrated only sixtythree), an astounding figure, no doubt ! Lastly, he has defined the alamkaras in his own way ; alamkara arises out of the fusion of varna and pada according to their respective qualities and symptoms. It is best expressed when the pada ultimately unites with the vakya (sentence, rather speech). The varnas are four, but according to the author of Vayupurana these are sthayi, sancari, arohi and abarohi, and not antara and abhog. These are accurately defined.

About the geetis, the author has also introduced new elements and terminology. For example, he has used the term 'bahirgeet' as different from the 'geet'. In the bahirgeet, he mentions, unconventional notes are applied. It may be assumed from the statement that a particular type of geeti has, for its unfoldment, a specific type of notes arranged in a definite pattern. If those specific notes are not used along the pattern the author does not consider it as a geeti ; it then becomes 'bahirgeet'. This is, of course, true in case of ragas in modern times. Does the author of Vayupurana mean thereby geeti as the raga ? Because, only in a raga specific notes are used in definite sequence. But he has, again, referred to the kind of geeti as madrak, that was mentioned by musicologists. However, Vayupurana gives us thereby ample materials as well as certain definite postulates to think in terms of reality.

Transition : A complete process

Viewed from such a historical perspective of Indian music, we find that only during the period just preceding that of Bharata, i.e., in the second stage of development, there was an attempt at systematization, because it was Bharata who, for the first time, referred to and dealt exhaustively with the jatis and its subdivisions on the one hand, and the dhruva, the earliest form of geetis on the other. That the jatis were themselves ragas or contained in them rudiments of ragas[1], is a matter of debatable discussion ; but studying the ten characteristics (dasa lakshamanas) of the jatis as mentioned by Bharata, there is left little doubt that these were the actual forerunners of the proper ragas. The svara structure, through a process of steady progression since the time of the early Vedas, came to a proper system with specific characteristics just referred to and took a more or less concrete shape so as to be termed ragas. As a parallel development, the song—the geeti as it was then called—took a proper shape in the form of dhruva. Besides dealing exhaustively with srutis, gramas, murchhanas, voice registers etc., Bharata treated, with the greatest importance, the jatis (jati ragas) and dhruva geetis in the twentyeighth to thirty-second chapters of the Natyasastra respectively. In fact, the entire thirty-second chapter is devoted to the discussion of dhruva geetis, with the few exclusion of twenty-five slokas where he discussed some other aspects relating to the characteristics of the veena player and the qualities of a musician, teacher, etc.

The discussion on the various aspects of Indian music then prevalent is quite systematic in the Natyasastra and one can easily guess to what maturity and emotive height the music reached at that time. Before the discussion on jatis, Bharata treated the seven notes, the two gramas and the srutis in the sadja and madhyama gramas, murchhanas and tans. Thus it may be seen that the constituents that led to the formation of jatis[2] are discussed in a chronological sequence. That the emergence of jatiragas is caused due to the mutual relation of notes as well as the development of such constituent elements, is quite evident from the nature of the description.

The base of all Indian music rests on the seven notes and Bharata named the notes sadja, rishava, gandhara, madhyama, pancama, dhaivata aud nishada, as *sapta ca svara* and in the very next sloka he mentioned the notes as belonging to four classes, e.g., vadi, samvadi, anuvadi and vivadi where the question of assonance and dissonance of notes has been discussed. This seems to be a very important point. Indian music, specially its classical forms, is based on melody-types, but the harmonic relationship between the notes is an integral part of the structural constituents of raga pattern. The very conception of vadi samvadi on the one hand and vivadi on the other rests on the principle of assonance, which relates to the essential harmonic nature of the constituent notes forming a raga pattern.

Along with the discussion on assonance and dissonance, the question of sruti becomes inevitable ; because, it is only in the discussion of the interval of notes that their relational aspects may be determined. It has been seen that the notes resting at a distance of eight and twelve sruti intervals, the assonance becomes most congenial and harmonic. That is why sadja is assonant with madhyama and pancama, and rishava with pancama, and so on. Bharata has admitted the existence of twenty-two srutis resting on the notes as follows :

Sadjascatusrutirgeya rishavastrisruti smrita
dwisrutiscapi gandharo madhyamasca catusruti
catusruti pancama syat trisrutidhaivata tatha
dwisrutistu naishadasyat sadjagrame swarantare.

This is true in respect of sadjagrama only. But in the madhyamagrama, the position of sruti has changed, dhaivata taking four and pancama three srutis. This is quite evident now, as madhyamagrama has become obsolete and the current practice of singing in sadjagrama having the above sruti intervals quite justifies the harmonic relationship that was established long ago. The relationship may be mathematically tabulated as follows :

sa	re	ga	ma	pa	dha	ni
4	3	2	4	4	3	2

more precisely, to put in mathematical proportion as follows :

sa : re : ga : : ma : : pa : dha : ni
4 : 3 : 2 : : 4 : : 4 : 3 : 2

Leaving aside the sruti interval from ma, or considering the entire gamut as composed of two tetrachords, the entire sequence is found to be quite harmonic.

Murchhanas have been described in detail and these are of fourteen kinds in the two gramas, the gandharagrama[3] being obsolete during the time of Bharata. The sadjagrama has seven murchhanas as

Uttaramandra	having notes as	S R G M P D N
Rajani	,,	N S R G M P D
Uttarayata	,,	D N S R G M P
Suddhasadja	,,	P D N S R G M
Asvakranta	,,	M P D N S R G
Matsarikrita	,,	G M P D N S R
Abhirudgata	,,	R G M P D N S

Manomohan Ghosh, in the Introduction to his translation of the Natyasastra, has observed a striking resemblance of the first six of these with the Greek modes Ionian, Dorian, Phrygian, Lydian, Mixolydian and Aeolian. The madhyamagrama has similarly given rise to seven murchhanas as Sauviri, Harinasva, Kalopanata, Suddhamadhya, Margavi, Pauravi and Hrishyaka, but in later years even the madhyamagrama became obsolete, the sadjagrama remaining the only grama for all practical purposes with definite sruti intervals as mentioned earlier. That the other two gramas became obsolete was due perhaps to their non-harmonic sruti divisions. The murchhanas in the sadjagrama were of four kinds according to the distribution of notes as sampurna, shadava, audava and sadharanikrita, the last one depending on the overlapping notes.

The modern concept of raga system, broadly described as melody-type, is the result of a long process of svara combination since the time of Bharata or even earlier. The successive discussion on svara, sruti, gramas and murchhanas and then on jatis clearly indicates that Bharata was conscious of the process which led to such a system resulting in the formation of melody-types. In the description of the Natyasastra, jatis and their subdivisions, sentiments and other attributes were focussed in every detail and one could guess that jatiragas might have been a living form of systematic music ; more than eleven centuries later when Sarangadeva discussed the ragas in the chapter on Ragadhyaya, he stressed importance on the jatiragas and their subdivisions no doubt, but that aspect was dealt with from a historical perspective. This is an indication of a prolonged and steady development of raga system that underwent many changes, fusion and intermixture. While Bharata mentions the term 'raga' only as associated with jatis, Sarangadeva devoted an exclusive chapter on the raga system. It is obvious therefrom that the term raga had found its constant and generalised use during his time and that jatiragas were a matter of a distant past. Bharata did not assign any definition to jati but mentioned how srutis led to the jatiragas. Catura Kallinatha, in his commentary on the Sangitratnakara, refers to the origin of jatis as

Gramadyayajjayata iti jataya

While Bharata attached more significance to srutis, Sarangadeva to the gramas. The word jati might have more than one significance of which two are vital for the determination of its character while discussing jatiragas. The first connotation relates to 'birth' when it might be assumed jatis to be of pure origin while the second connotation as 'classification' might refer jatis to be of certain broad classes from which later jatis originated.

In the Natyasastra Bharata did not treat ragas separately though he mentioned the term[4] on more than one occasion. In the slokas from 38 to 151 he had dealt with jatis quite exhaustively and assigned their origin, mentioned their characters, classification and finally gave description of the eighteen suddha and vikrita jatis. It is obvious, therefore, that the term raga did not find any generalised use during his time. In the 29th chapter where he discussed the alamkaras and rasas, there even ragas were not mentioned in relation to evocative sentiments. There are good number of reasons that might lead one to guess that raga was not something different from the jatis. Not only the ragas were later development of the jatis, jatiragas and gramaragas but also the characteristics which go to define a raga were the same that were ascribed to the jatis. The following reasons might prove that the ragas were the same as the jatiragas of earlier periods if certain characteristics are taken into consideration :

Bharata mentions as tenpoint characteristics of a jati

dasabidham jatilakshmanam

it is further mentioned

Grahamsau taramandrau ca nyasapanyasa eba ca
alpatvam ca bahutvam ca shadavauduvite tatha

the characteristics are graha, amsa, tar, mandra, nyasa, apanyasa, alpatva, bahutva, shadava and audava. These characteristics are still assigned to the raga in the modern period while determining its quality. Bharata then explained all these characteristics in separate slokas.

The jatis have been classified as suddha and vikrita. In modern times even ragas have three broad categories as suddha, shalaga and samkirna. The vikrita jatis have been originated by a process of fusion and mixture, so have the samkirna ragas been derived that way.

The shadava audava characters of the jatis are also the

specific characters of the ragas in modern times. The hexatonic or pentatonic notes used in certain ragas determine their characters as shadava or audava.

The ragas used to tinge or colour and to evoke corresponding sentiments in human mind and so also the jatis. Bharata describes in detail in the 29th chapter of Natyasastra all these emotive attributes. The erotic, comic, heroic, furious, marvellous, pathetic, terrible, odious, etc., are the sentiments that the jatis can evoke[5]. He further mentions 'only the sadjamadhya is the jati which can accommodate all the sentiments'.

The ragas, in modern times, are applied to songs and so were the jatis. The usage of four varnas could also be found in the Natyasastra :

arohi cabarohi ca sthaisancarinau tatha

while discussing the relation between jati and raga, the above points should be considered. As Swami Prajnanananda has stated[6], the term raga was used though only on a few occasions, yet these eighteen suddha and vikrita jatis were perpaps nothing but ragas with powers to excite emotion and pleasing sentiments.

It was a long process of fusion, mixture and separation until we arrive at the modern concept of raga. The process elaborately categorises such terms as jatiragas, gramaragas, bhasa, bibhasa, antarabhasa etc., but this long chain had certain permanent aspects common to them and the modern concept of raga ingrained within it the basic constituents that went into its complete and artistic blending.

The jatis, before and at the time of Bharata, were divided into two classes, suddha and vikrita (pure and modified). In the sadjagrama, there were four pure jatis as sadji, arshavi, dhaivati and naishadi while in the madhyamagrama those were gandhari, madhyama and pancami. The pure jatis consisted of all the notes having amsa, graha and nyasa. The modified jatis were eleven in number and grew out of combinations from the pure jatis. These were sadjakaisiki, sadjadicyava, sadja-madhya, raktagandhari, gandharodicyava, gandharapancami, madhyamodicyava, andhri, nandayanti, karmaravi and kaisiki. The description and characteristics of each of these jatis were elaborately given in the N. S. An English rendering by Manomohan Ghosh reads as : Sadji, 'In the sadji jati, the amsa is of five notes (of the grama), nishada and rishava being excluded. Its apanyasa is gandhara and pancama, and nyasa, sadja ; and nishada should be dropped from it. Its hexatonic treatment should exclude nishada. In it, dhaivata and nishada should be reduced ; and sadja and gandhara as well as dhaivata and sadja should move together, and gandhara should be amplified. These jatis with ten characteristics should be applied in the song (pada) with dance movements (karanas) and gestures suitable to them. The four kinds of songs or geetis in which the jatis were applied were magadhi, ardhamagadhi, sambhavita and prithula.'

While the above kinds of geetis considered the pada and tala more than anything else and applied to jatis, the five kinds of geetis that developed at a later period as suddha, vinna, goudi, besara and sadharani considered the raga element more systematically and were applied to the gramaragas. Saranga-deva referred to the jatiragas from the historian's point of view, but treated gramaragas and their offshoots in all detail as the existing order of the day. Rajyeswar Mitra, in his commentary on the Ratnakara has made the following observation[7] : the raga based itself on the geetis and in the process, the geetis have emerged from the poetic to the musical world [tr. by the author].

The gramaragas, thirty in number, based themselves on the above the geetis in both the gramas ; as seven in the suddha geeti, five in the vinna geeti, three in the goudi geeti, eight in the besara geeti and seven in the sadharani geeti. A few raga names that are in use even in the present times find a place in the above list, as Hindol based on besara geeti, Kukuv on the sadharani geeti, etc. Hindol, at present, uses vikrita madhyam while Kukuv uses all the suddha notes with vikrita nishada in the descending order, being itself a variety of Bilawal.

After the gramaragas there are eight uparagas in the series. The names of these uparagas are all obsolete now as is evident from the list : Sakatilaka, Rebagupta, Kokilapancama, etc. The next list relates to the ragas which are twenty in number as Sree, Natta, Nattanarayan, Bhairab, Megh, Kamod (two varieties), Desakhya (Debsakh ?), Bhas, Madhyamsharab, Raktahanasa, Kohlhas, Prasab, Dhani, Som, Amrapancam, Kandarpa, Bangal (two varieties), Kaisikkukuv. Of these Sree, Nat (in union with other ragas as Chhaya, Bhairab, etc.), Bhairab, Megh, Kamod are in general use, Desakhya (Debsakh ?) and Bangal (in union with Bhariab) are rare, while the rest are obsolete completely. Dhani is also a rare raga if not completely obsolete. Bibhas might be the modern form of Bhas. There are two kinds of Bibhas now in use, one in the Bilawal thata and other in the Bhairaba thata, pentatonic in scale. While in the earlier variety all the suddha notes are used, in the second category, komal R and komal D are used excluding the notes M N, which means Bhupali scale with komal R and komal D.

The gramaragas are again classified into three categories according to their nature of alapa. These classes are also termed ragas as bhasa, bibhasa and antarabhasa. The bhasas are ninety-six in number, bibhasa twenty and antarabhasas only four. A few names are still in use. The kukuva gramaraga has given rise to kambhoji bhasa. The kambhoji raga is not current in the North Indian system, but is very popular in the South Indian style. The name has affinity with khambaj with komal N in the descending order. The takka gramaraga has given rise to lalita bhasa. Lalita (Lalit ?) might be the modern form of Lalit, an early morning raga using both suddha and tivra madhyam in succession. While gouri bhasa has come from the Malabakausik gramaraga (Malkaus ?), the gandhari bhasa has descended from gandharapancam gramaraga. Both these bhasaragas are now not uncommon. Gouri belongs to the Purvi thata with komal R, komal D and tivra M, while Gandhari is quite akin to Jaunpuri. This raga is not obsolete but rare with G D N komal notes. These are the only bhasaragas which have their raga patterns preserved even in modern times.

The gramaragas, their offshoots bhasa, bibhasa and antara-bhasas got mixed up during a long process and developed along the popular tunes retaining a systematic form of progression. This fusion and mixing up once gave rise to the broad classification as deshi ragas that might be termed as the forerunner of all the modern ragas. Just before the time of Sarangadeva, Locana kavi, the court musician of King Ballalsena of Bengal (1160 A D. approx.) composed Ragtarangini where he mentioned twelve basic ragas termed as *janaka* ragas from which originated eighty-six derivative ragas, *janya.* It is seen, therefore, that the conception of modern raga and its system already took a shape about the time of Locana kavi, before the advent of Sarangadeva. It may be assumed that the later formulation of thata and the raga system of Indian classical music was but a development of the *janaka-janya* relation of raga music prevalent during the time of Locana kavi. In fact, the credit of systematization goes to him.

The so-called deshi ragas mentioned by Sarangadeva gave rise to other raga varieties as raganga, bhasanga, kriyanga and upanga out of which he made two broad generalizations as Purva-prasiddha and Adhuna-prasiddha, meaning probably thereby that some of those were prevalent in ancient times and the rest were current in his own time. Strangely enough, the total number of such varieties as raganga, bhasanga, kriyanga and upanga was eighty-six which did exactly corroborate with the figure of janya ragas mentioned by Locana kavi. It is quite possible that Sarangadeva was aware of Locana kavi's Ragtarangini and he might have consulted it[8] to describe those eighty-six janya ragas mentioned by Locana ;

Sarangadeva himself admitted that not only he tried to explain what he did find new but also described and summarized the findings of his predecessors. Or, it may further be contended that the development of raga music was already coming to a definite standardization and the total number of such new ragas, born out of fusion and mixture, was specific and determined even at that time and was known to leading musicologists throughout the country. Whatever might be the exact version, it may be ascertained that the janya ragas mentioned by Locana kavi were of the same nature as those mentioned by Sarangadeva as raganga, bhasanga, kriyanga and upanga. These were possibly the ultimate subdivisions or forms of individual specific ragas, demonstrated by the musicians.

Sarangadeva gives a list of such varieties in detail. There are a few names in the Purva-prasiddha raganga which are familiar to us but not in current use. Dipak is one such. Sankarabharan is a basic raga in the Carnatik system of South Indian music. Chhaya [Chhayanat is prevalent, Chhaya[9] is not so common these days] belongs to the bhasanga type. The names belonging to the kriyanga and upanga varieties are now completely unfamiliar. The raga varieties belonging to the Adhuna-prasiddha series are mentioned as Madhyamadi (Sarang ?), Todi, Bangal (Bhairab ?), Bhairab, Barati, Gurjari (Todi), Gour (Malhar), Kolahal, Basantak (Basanta ?), Dhanyasi, (Dhanasri ?), Deshi, Desakhya (Debsakh ?). Excepting the raga Kolahal, all other raga varieties are still known, a few are quite popular even these days. Madhyamadi or Madhumadhabi is a variety of the broad raga Sarang, Bangal is a type of Bhairab, Gurjari is a form of Todi, Gour might be a separate raga which did exist in earlier times, but it is now current as Gour Malhar. The bhasanga varieties did contain Belabali (Bilawal ?) Natta (Nat), Nagadhvani (Kanada). The others are completely unheard these days while the last-named is also obscure though the name is familiar as a form of Kanada. Of the three kriyanga ragas mentioned by Sarangadeva,

Ramkriti (Ramkeli ?) is still current and quite popular as Ramkeli with komal D and tivra M. Among the other twentyseven upanga ragas mentioned by him, there are six varieties of Barati, two of Todi, four of Gurjari[10]. Only the names as Bhairabi, Chhayanatta (Chhayanat) Ramkriti (Ramkeli ?), Mallari (Malhar), Gour Malhar are now current.

The entire list is quite significant for more than one perspective. Firstly, it may be seen that out of the list of eighty-six specific varieties of deshi ragas only twenty-two ragas are now heard of. Even among these twenty-two, a few again are not in current use, while the present number of ragas including both popular and uncommon types runs into more than two hundred. This clearly signifies that the raga music in India is a tremendously dynamic form of practising art not, however, without a sociological content, as a number of raga names do signify. It has created and recreated itself time and again and has not lost itself into the domain of dry history only. While a great number of ragas have gone out of practice, a greater number have originated since the time of Sarangadeva during these last seven centuries. This has been possible due to creation as well as fusion, amalgamation, mixing up and such other processes.

Secondly, tribal influence might have gone a long way in the formative stage of development of Indian ragas. To quote O.C.Gangooly from his article, 'Non-Aryan Contribution to Indian Music'[11], Aryan or Indian music has grown and developed by appropriating and assimilating a large body of aboriginal elements which existed long before the growth of the characteristic Indian system. He further refers to Brihaddesi where the source of a large number of ragas is stated to be aboriginal. Those were Takka, Takka-kaisika, Ahiri, Malava-kaisika (later named as Malkaus), Malava-Pancam, Gurjari and Pulindi. Takka is a gramaraga in the sadja-grama based on Besara geeti, Kaisika was quite popular a form as evinced from the fact that as gramaraga it based all the forms of prevalent geetis and as many as nine varieties of Kaisika belonged to those geetis. Ahiri (Abhiri ?) and Gurjari are bhasa ragas belonging to the gramaraga Pancam. These names obviously refer to the tribal influence during the formative stage of raga development.

Thirdly, the regional culture and musical heritage of certain places did cast their influence on the process of development of Indian ragas. Local popular tunes probably got mixed up with certain ragas and formed new varieties. Sourashtri is a bhasaraga belonging to the gramaraga Takka ; Andhri and Dakshinatya are two other bhasa ragas belonging to the gramaraga Pancam, Bangali and Gour are two bhasa ragas belonging to Malavakaisik gramaraga. Four upanga ragas as Maharashtri-Gurjari, Sourashtri-Gurjari, Dakshina-Gurjari and Dravida-Gurjari are direct evidences of such raga-formation through the admixture of local tunes. All the above ragas have derived their names from important localities of India and that the names of the ragas have been current by those names quite conclusively proves of such influence.

1. Simhabhupala, in his commentary on the Sangitratnakara, observed as follows :

Sakalasya ragaderjanmahetutvajjayata

2. Manomohan Ghosh has observed in his translation of the Natyasastra (Asiatic Society Publication) :

'But jatis are the primitive melody-types from which ragas of later Hindu music developed. Jati meaning 'birth' probably stands here for recognised melody-types of the day, which were considered to be of (pure) birth as opposed to other types which were hybrids.

3. The sruti division of Gandhara and Madhyamagrama is as follows :

G grama	S R G M P D N	3 2 4 3 3 3 4
M grama	S R G M P D N	4 3 2 4 3 4 2

4. Swami Prajnanananda: Sangit O Samskriti, p. 272.

5. Translation of Natyasastra by Manomohan Ghosh, pp. 29-30.

6. Swami Prajnanananda : Sangit O Samskriti, p. 279.

7. Rajyeswar Mitra : Sangit Samiksha, p. 95.

8. Sarangadeva mentioned of nearabout thirty musicologists before his time and whose contribution to the theory and knowledge of music he did uphold in great esteem qualifying them as Sangitbisharads. But he did not mention the name of Ragtarangini nor its author Locana kavi who had lived much before his time.

9. Ustad Faiyaz Khan used to sing Chhaya and has a disc record in Chhaya drut trital.

10. In the list of ragas in the adhuna-prasiddha series there is Todi as well as Gurjari. Moreover, there is found a variety of Gurjari which signifies that the latter was not only a distinct but important raga.

11. Annals of the Bhandarker Oriental Research Institute, pt. 3, Vol. XIX, 1938.

Naradiyasiksha : A prelude to Natyasastra

Before entering into the study of Natyasastra, an approach to the Naradiyasiksha would be proper for a scientific as well as chronological study of the history of ancient music in India. While accepting the date of the Siksha as approximately first century A.D., Swami Prajnanananda definitely observes[1] that the Siksha is an earlier treatise than the Natyasastra of Bharata. Manomohan Ghose, while editing Bharata's Natyasastra, observes the following in his 'nivedanam' :

Natyasastrasya dvitiyabhagasya shatsu adhyaeshu kebalang (chs. 28-33) gitavadyam alocitam. Naradiyasikshang bihaya etadeva hi sangitasastrabishayam pracinatamamalocitam.

Of the two editions of the book, the one edited by Samagacarya Satyabrata Samasrami is older. The other annotated version edited by Pandit Bhattasovakar appeared later. This small book on music containing only 230 slokas (ed : Satyabrata Samasrami) is, however, of much importance to the scholars even today. Firstly, it deals with all the relevant topics that are included in music proper ; secondly, it narrates both the vedic and laukika svaras in detail and lastly, it establishes a relationship between the vedic and laukika svaras. Considering the above aspects, Naradiyasiksha has found a permanent place in the history of musicology, and has surpassed the other sikshas, as Paniniya, Jajnabalkya or Manduki in importance.

The sikshas primarily deal with svara and chhanda of the vedic mantras. It may be found in the pratisakhyas that svara itself has been connoted as brahmana and that it should be attained first in order to reach the ultimate stage of parama brahman. Oudabraji, considered to be the author of Rikpratisakhya, has mentioned three different stages in the development of the samagana. In the Pushpasutras, however, the various modes of singing, according to different branches of the samagana, are referred. In the Suklajajupratisakhya, there is specific explanation of the hrasva, dirgha and pluta svaras, corresponding to the three various degrees in time-scheme.

Panini, on the other hand, approached the problem of svara and its evolution from a philosophical standpoint. His explanation has possibly found an echo in the writings of Sarangadeva long afterwards when he has dealt with the same problem in the sloka :

atma bibakshamanohyang manah prerayatey manah
dehasthang bahnimahanti sa prerayati marutam

[tr : This Atman, having a desire to speak, stirs the mind. The mind stirs the fire abiding in the body. That (fire) strikes the wind]. The strange parallelism may be found if we consider the earlier sloka in the Siksha :

manah kayagnimahanti sa prerayati marutam

Jajnabalkya's approach to the problem was, however, spiritual but Manduk'siksha's concern related to the application of svaras. He stated that all the seven notes were applicable in the samagana. It may be noted, however, that the number of notes varied according to the various branches of samagana in earlier times.

Narada, on the other hand, discussed the problem from a broad perspective. He laid emphasis on the rules of svara-sastra, but he did not forget to mention about the alamkars that a musician should take note of. Rather, he was conscious that the music should be approached from an aesthetic standpoint. His was a complete view and in less than only one hundred and sixteen slokas in the first *prapathaka* he has summed up a comprehensive view of ancient Hindu music.

There is, of course, some differences of opinion amongst the scholars about the existence of a particular Narada. There are a number of musical treatise that have been ascribed to his name. Scholars differ in viewing that there was only one Narada. That there were at least two, respectively of the Siksha and of Makaranda, is generally accepted. Internal evidences have led to the conclusion that Narada, the author of Makaranda, lived round about the tenth century.

Narada, at the beginning of his Siksha, has referred to music as svarasastra thereby emphasizing the utmost importance of svara. He admits, at the same time, that music is the result of a long and sustained pursuit for ages resulting in the formation of a sastra as such. The svara development as arcika, gathika, samika and svarantarita is mentioned. The logical acumen of the author is revealed when he speaks of bisvara which results from unscientific pursuit of music.

The vedic notes are prathama, dvitiya, tritiya, caturtha, mandra, krushta, atisvara, as used in the samagana. The sequence of the notes as revealed in the sloka,

Prathamasca dvitiyasca tritiyohtha catruthakah
mandra krushto atisvara etan kurbanti samagah

lead to some confusion. Krushta succeeds atisvara and that is why the corresponding laukika note pancam comes in the sequence as, D, N, P, in the abaroha (descending) order as stated by some musicologists [The present author has discussed about this sequence elsewhere in this book in details].

The music materials of the period were

tanaragasvaragramamurchhananang

which were sacred and beneficial according to Narada. Then he elaborates the famous principle that guides the tonal structure as

Saptasvarastrayograma murchhanstekabingsati
tana ekonapancasadityetat Svaramandalam

the seven svaras, three gramas, twenty-one murchhanas, forty-nine tanas constitute the svaramandal. The last word is quite significant as it reflects Narada's total comprehension of music as an entire process revealed through the application of svaras. In the next sloka he mentions the seven laukika svaras as sadja, rishava, gandhara, madhyama, pancama, dhaivata and nishada.

Narada's analysis of the vedic as well as his reference to laukika svaras reveals that the author existed at a time when samaganas had become part of history and the laukika music was in practice. The gandhara grama of which he speaks as having rested on the svaragaloka (heaven) was also out of date. but sadja and madhyama grama existed in the bhuloka and bhuvarloka :

Bhurlokajjayatey sadjo bhubarlokacca madhyamah

Bhuloka signifies the earth where music is practised in the sadja grama, but the actual significance of bhuvarloka remains partly in a veil of mystery. As legend goes, bhuvarloka is conceived as a place in between the heaven and the earth. Legend goes that gandharvas lived in a region, unapproachable to the common man and it was there that they practised their music. The area, high up in the mountains, may be termed bhuvarloka where they could took to singing in the madhyama grama ! Did madhyamagrama then really exist for the common man ?

Narada places the forty-nine tanas as under :

Madyhamagrama 20, Sadjagrama 14, Gandharagrama 15. The seven murchhanas in the sadja grama corresponding to the notes SRGMPDN are uttaramandra, abhirudgata, asvakranta, soubira, hrisyaka, uttarayata and rajani.[2] The author conceives of various deities, colours etc., as attributes to the respective svaras. The deities of sadja and nishada, the first and last svara of the sequence are God and the Yaksha. While the colour of sadja resembles that of the petals of the lotus, that of nishada is a combination of all colours. Like deity and colour, he has also attributed caste to the svaras, e.g., sadja, madhyama and gandhara are Brahmins etc.

But what is really significant is his description of the ten qualities or characteristics of music. The passage reads as :

ganasya tu dashavidha gunavrittistadjatha
raktang purna malankritang prasannang byaktang bikrustang
slakshnang samang sukumarang madhura miti gunah

The passage has also been annotated properly by the author in subsequent lines. Bharata as well as Sarangadeva have attributed similar qualities and a detailed reference and critical estimate would be made later, in the chapters on Sangit-ratnakara.

Swami Prajnanananda, in his important treatise,[3] has quoted an extensive passage from the Naradiyasiksha to describe the seven gramaragas that existed during Narada's time. Those are sadja grama, madhyama, madhyamagrama, pancama, sadharita, kaisika, kaisikamadhyama. In the description of sadja gramaraga, Narada clarifies that the application of nishada would be subtle, that of gandhara be prominent, while that of dhaivata would be trembling. The word kampita

Dhaivatah kampita jatra

leaves one in doubt. Did it mean "andolita" as in modern practice we find the application of Komal R in Bhairab or Komal G in Darbari Kanada ? However, Narada emphatically describes the other gramaragas with their specific applications of the laukika notes.

The most important slokas in the Naradiyasiksha run as :

Jah samaganang prathamah sa benormadhyamah svarah
Jo divitiya sa gandharastritiyastrishavah smritah
caturthah sadja ityahuh pancama dhaivato bhavet
sastho nishado bijneya saptamah pancamah smritah

Narada, for the first time, established the relation between the vedic and laukika notes, the pancama, shashtha and saptama of the vedic notes being termed originally as mandra, atisvara and krushta. The relative sequence has already been shown in chapter III [Transformations : Stage III p. 25]. This finding is of immense importance because of the following factors :

1. The continuity of the development of ancient music was established.

2. The exact relationship between the vedic and laukika svaras could be traced.

3. The vedic notes, in relation to the laukika ones, were found to be in the descending order.

4. The order of the vedic notes were not simple and straight but of a curved nature [bakra or bankim gati].

That the laukika notes as sadja etc., resembled the utterances of various birds and animals were referred to by many other musicologists. The theme was so commonly accepted in those days that the poets also made use of the reference. Kalidasa, in his classical work Raghuvamsam, cites such an example :

Sadjasambadini keka

Narada just states the traditional theory here. But, in a later sloka, refers to the instruments that were in use during the vedic period. Those were darabi and gatra veena. He also mentions the technique of handling them with accuracy.

Narada's concept of sruti is highly poetical and he uses grand simile to focus the relation of sruti with svara :

Jathapsu caratang margo minanang nopalabhyatey
akasey ba bihanganang tatabatsvaragata srutih
Jatha dadhani sarpih syat kasthastho ba jathanalah
prajatney nopalabhyatey tatbatsvaragata srutih

[As the fish swims in the water and the birds fly over the sky, the sruti follows the svara in the same way ; further, it has the same relation as the serpent with the milk or the fire with the wood]. These srutis again are classified within the five jatis as dipta, ayata, karuna, mridu and madhya.

Narada has referred to Tumburu, Vasistha, Bisvabasu as earlier exponents. He has accepted music as an art that has to be learnt from the guru or acharya. It reveals that Narada was not only a great theoretician, but an expert in the practical art also who could reveal such an insight.

1. Swami Prajnanananda : Bharatiya Sangiter Itihas.
3. This list of names and sequence of the murchhanas in the sadjagrama does not campletely tally with those mentioned by Bharata.
3. Swami Prajnanananda : Bharatiya Sangiter Itihas.

The Natyasastra

A span of almost four hundred years has been tentatively fixed by the scholars as to the period during which BharataMuni might have composed the slokas of Natyasastra. Manomohan Ghosh, while editing the treatise, accepts Haraprasad Sastri's conclusion that the work belonged to 200 B. C. While Swami Prajnanananda quotes, in his text, Dr. Raghavan's view that the upper age limit of Bharata might be taken as the second century B.C., he himself admits that the text was written at about the second century A.D. There is doubt also as to the existence of a particular Bharata. It has been expressed by many that Bharata is not a particular sage, but a general title and as many as five Bharatas are recorded in various texts. At least, the existence of Brahma Bharata cannot be doubted. He composed some thirty-six thousand slokas for his Natyaveda. Scholars also differ on the total number of slokas in Bharata's Natyasastra which incorporates something between six and twelve thousand slokas. The present writer is, however, concerned with the few chapters that Bharata wrote to illustrate the music of his time. There are a total number of one thousand six hundred and fortyeight slokas in the six adhyayas [28th—33rd chapters]. More than one thousand slokas are devoted to the chapters on tala and dhruva geetis. The chapter on susira contains only thirteen slokas.

It may be remembered at the outset that the music Bharata dealt with, was primarily applied to the drama. In the third sloka of chapter 28, he clearly states that the musical insturments have specific application in relation to the drama :

prayogastribidho jhyeshang bijjnayo natakasraya

and again :

dhrubabidhaney kartabya jatigana (*prajoktrivih*)

This will clearly be exemplified later, in the chapter on dhruva geetis, when he writes on the pravesiki, akshepiki, prasadiki, antara and naishkramiki as the various forms [Sts. 26-27 Ch. 32].

Bharata starts with the 'adotyavidhim' meaning thereby instrumental music, that are of four kinds as tata (stringed), avanaddha (covered), ghana (solid) and sushira (hollow). The examples of these four kinds may be cited as veena, drums or tala instruments (mridanga), khanjani, karatal, and flute, respectively. The next important observation relates to the orchestration. A band of singers (the main singer and his attendants) and the players of vipanci, veena and flute constitute the orchestral combine that Bharata termed as

Kutapabinyasa

There is another variety of kutapa with the covered instruments as mridanga, panava and dardura ; kutapabinyasa may be arranged in three different ways as uttama, madhya and adhama, depending on the number of persons engaged. Bharata refers to the artistic unity of the song, the instrumental music and the acting, a perfect understanding of which makes the production highly satisfying. The next sloka is important from the historical aspect.

He describes gandharva sangita :

Jattu tantrikritang proktang nanatodyasamasrayam
gandharvamiti tajgeyang svaratalapadasrayam

[That which is made by the stringed instruments and depends (as well) on various other instruments, and consists of notes (svara), tala (time-measure) and verbal themes (pada) should be known as the Gandharva]. These songs are much desired by the gods and give pleasure to the gandharvas.

In the next few slokas Bharata describes the scope of his work and refers to the various aspects of the veena, of the human throat, of the padas and talas. While padas are of two kinds as anibaddha and nibaddha, there are as many as twenty formal aspects of tala. There are seven svaras : sadja, rishabha, gandhara, madhyama, pancama, dhaivata and nishada, which are of four classes : vadi, samvadi, anuvadi and vivadi.

Vadi(n) is also called the amsa svara [an exhaustive reference to amsa svara may be found later]. The note that falls on the ninth or the thirteenth sruti from the vadi is called its samvadi [the two being mutually consonant]. In the madhyamagrama, pancama and rishabha are consonant, in the sadjagrama, sadja with pancama. The notes that are at an interval of two or twenty srutis are called dissonant as gandhara and madhyama, sadja and nishada. After describing the assonant notes in the two gramas as sadja and madhyama, Bharata refers to twenty-two srutis which are arranged as :

In the Sadjagrama :

S 4, R 3, G 2, M 4, P 4, D 3, N 2 ;

,, ,, Madhyama grama :

S 4, R 3, G 2, M 4, P 3, D 4, N 2 ;

And that D takes one sruti from P in the madhyamagrama is detailed by the author in the line

madhyamagramey tu srutyapakrishtah pancama karyyah

[In the madhyamagrama pancama should be made deficient in one sruti]. He then follows up by describing pramana (unit) sruti. It is evident that the idea of a sruti or that of pramana sruti is purely subjective and depends on the accuracy of a particular musician in differentiating the relative degree, pitch and intensity of sound.

The murchhanas in the two gramas are[1] :

First Note	Sadjagrama	First note	Madhyamagrama
Sadja	Uttaramandra	Madhyama	Sauviri
Nishada	Rajani	Gandhara	Harinasva
Dhaivata	Uttarayata	Rishabha	Kalopanata
Pancama	Suddhasadja	Sadja	Suddhamadhya
Madhyama	Matsarikrita	Nishada	Margavi
Gandhara	Asvakranta	Dhaivata	Pauravi
Rishabha	Abhirudgata	Pancama	Hrishyaka

These two lines are very important for a comparative study of the notes of both the sadjagrama and the madhyamagrama :

1) *asang sadjanishada dhaivatapancamamadhyama gandhara-rishavah adya svarah sadjagramey*

2) *asang madhyamagandhararishavasadjanishadadhaivata-pancamah anupurbadyah svarah madhyamagramey*

The murchhanas were vitally connected with the concept of grama during Bharata's time. The gramas were so named possibly because the primary murchhanas as Uttaramandra and Sauviri started with the sadja in the sadjagrama and with madhyama in the madhyamagrama respectively.

The seven notes taken together in order of succession form a complete murchhana while the series with six or five notes are called shadava and oudava. Manomohan Ghosh has specifically referred to the tanas in his translation of the sloka 33, but Bharata has not used the word tana exclusively, rather pointed out, in a succeeding passage

murchhanasangsritastanascaturasiti

It may be concluded, however, that the tanas in the modern context are but later development of the murchhanas. [Narada in his siksha has referred to tanas along with murchhana]. Murchhanas were

kramajukta

i.e., in order or succession. Tanas had to depend on the murchhanas as evident from the sloka ; but in modern practice, a tana should not necessarily be in succession of ascending or descending notes. It is only in the case of simple tanas that the order or sequence is maintained properly. In other cases as the kuta tana, alamkarik tana etc., the order is maintained in a variety of ways, ignoring completely the descending or ascending pattern in succession.

The next sloka relates to murchhanas of a different kind, with kakali orantarasvara. These relate to overlapping notes. When gandhara normally takes two srutis of madhyama and nishada takes those of sadja, i.e., when G and N overlap on their successive svaras partly, these are termed as antara gan-dhara and kakali nishada. The sense of overlapping notes

Bharata poetically describes by comparing these with the changing season in sloka 35 [Neither has the spring come (fully) nor has the winter gone away completely].

Bharata next goes on to describe jatis, the most intriguing subject in ancient music. There are 18 jatis in the two gramas, 7 in the sadjagrama and 11 in the madhyamagrama. Of these total of eighteen, 7 jatis owe their names to the 7 notes, and these are pure, meaning thereby that these have amsa, graha and nayasa,

Sadja grama	*Madhyama grama*
Sadji	Gandhari
Arshabhi	Raktagandhari
Dhaivati	Gandharodicyava
Naishadi	Madhyamadicyava
	Madhyama
Sadjakaisiki	Pancama
Sadjamadhyama	Gandharapancami
Sadjodicyavati	Andhri
	Nandyayanti
	Karmaravi
	Kaisiki

The rest, i.e., eleven arising out of combination are modified (vikrita) jatis, which lack two or more of characteristics except the nyasa,

jatayo dvibidha suddha bikritasca...
parasparang sangjogadekadasa nirbartayanti.

The formation of the vikrita jatis is detailed below :

Vikrita Jatis	*Combination of*
Sadjakaisiki	Sadji and Gandhari
Sadjamadhyama	Sadji and Madhyama
Sadjodicyava	Sadji, Gandhari and Dhaivati
Andhri[2]	Gandhari and Arshabhi

The sloka reads as ;

gandharisadjabhyang sangsargajjayate candhri

Gandharapancami	Gandhari and Pancami
Nandyayanti	Gandhari, Pancami and Arshabhi
Karmaravi	Naishadi, Arshabhi and Pancami
Gandharodicyava	Gandhari, Sadji, Dhaivati and Madhyama
Madhyamadicyava	Gandhari, Madhyama, Pancami and Dhaivati
Raktagandhari	Gandhari, Pancami, Naishadi and Madhyama
Kaisiki	Sadji, Gandhari, Madhyama, Pancami, Naishadi [combination of all the pure jatis excepting Arshabhi and Dhaivati]

The arrangement of the vikrita jatis in the first column has been slightly modified from that of the text of Natyasastra. It would be seen that the first three relate to sadja grama, the rest eight to madhyama grama In the vikrita series, the jatis are arranged in order of their combining with two, three, four and five jatis in sequence. The combination pattern as shown in the right-hand column has been left undisturbed. This is just for convenience. Bharata, of course, maintains the relative sequence. It may be seen that gandhari is the most important pure jati which had gone in combination on as many as nine occasions to form nine different vikrita jatis. This is interesting to remember that gandhara had also been the most important svara in all the three gramas. A few other points are also important for consideration. The jatis in the sadja grama do not combine among themselves, while those in the madhyama grama do unite to form vikrita jatis. Moreover, one or more jati or jatis of the madhyama grama combines or combine with one or two pure jatis belonging to sadja grama. Of these, four are heptatonic (with seven svaras), four are hexatonic (with six svaras) and the rest ten are pentatonic (with five svaras). The heptatonic are Sadjakaisiki (sadja grama), Madhyamadicyava, Gandharapancami and Karmaravi (madhyama grama).

There are ten characteristics of the jati, according to Bharata :

dasabidhang jatilakshamanam
grahangsau taramandrau ca nasapanyasa eba ca
alpatvang ca bahutvang ca shadabaurubitey tatha

[Ten characteristics of the jatis are : Graha, Amsa, Tara, Mandra, Nyasa, Apanyasa, Reduction (Alpatva), Amplification (Bahutva), hexatonic treatment (Shadava), and pentatonic treatment (Audavita)].

In the succeeding slokas Bharata describes the ten lakshmanas, stressing due importance on the amsa, the note on which the charm of a song depends (the ranjana sakti). The following are the amsa svaras of the various jatis :

Jati	*Amsa and Graha Svaras*
Sadji	Sadja, gandhara, madhyama, pancama and dhaivata
Arshavi	Rishabha, dhaivata and nishada
Gandhrai	Rishabha, gandhara, madhyama, pancama and nishada
Madhyama	Rishabha, sadja, madhyama, pancama, dhaivata
Dhaivati	Dhaivata, Rishabha
Pancami	Rishabha, Pancama
Naishadi	Rishabha, gandhara, Nishada

There is little difference between Amsa and Graha svaras for practical purposes, as Bharata himself admits that 'Amsas are always Grahas in all these Jatis'.

The above list relates to the pure jatis only. While pancama the only amsa as well as Graha svara of Madhyamadicyava, Nandyayanti and Gandharapancami, all the seven svaras are used as amsa svaras in the Sadjamadhyama jati. It may be concluded from the above list that :

1. The Jatis are named after that particular note where Nyasa is used at the end ; (the sequence is altered in the list

for convenience) ; as, in Sadji jati, the nyasa is sadja ; in Arshavi jati, the nyasa is Rishabha and so on ;

2. The particular svara is also present as one of the amsa svaras ;

3. The number of amsa svara varies from one to seven in the various jatis ;

4. The sequence as maintained by Bharata starts from the jati, having one svara as its amsa ;

5. Amsas are always grahas in all the jatis. While nyasa occurs at the end of a song, the apanyasa may be used within the song proper.

Bharata has given definite indication of two very important points, i.e., antaramarga and sancara, while discussing alpatva and bahutva respectively. The referenee to antaramarga suggests that the song might have more than one structural division, while sancara signifies that the song proper had a freedom of movement and was not a closed pada. The ten characteristics are to be applied to the song suitably. Bharata concludes the 28th chapter by referring to two most important topics that are related to the aesthetic as well as historical aspect of ancient music :

ebameto budhuirjneya jatayo dasalaksmanah,
svaih svaisca karanairjojya padesvabhinayairapi

[These are jatis with their ten characteristics. These should be applied in the song (pada) with dance movements (karanas) and gestures suitable to them].

And lastly he suggests to discuss their specific application in relation to rasa and bhava in the next chapter.

Manomohan Ghosh, while explaining the first sloka of chapter 29, makes the following comment, which needs careful study : "As songs, included in the performance of a play, were to serve its principal purpose which was the evocation of sentiments, the author discusses here how jatis can be applied for this purpose. The seven notes which have already been assigned in different sentiments, played an important part in this connexion. All these ultimately led to the formation of the ragas of the later Indian music, in which the particular melody-types were meant not only to create a sentiment appropriate to a situation in a play, but also to act on the hearers' emotion in such a way that they might experience in imagination the particular situations described in isolated songs as well" (N.S., P. 28). Two points become clear from the above comment. The ragas in Indian music were a later formation and that these ragas could evoke proper sentiments. Moreover, it was given also an objective character because of its power of reproducing an imagination that might well lead to the understanding of a particular situation, i.e., the dramatic quality could be found latent in a raga. With all these in view someone may find a better approach to Bharata's treatment of the sentiments as applied to the jatis.

That each particular note is responsible for evoking specific sentiment is laid down in the following sloka :

hasya sringarayoh karyau svarau madhyamapancamau
sadjarishavau ca kartabyau biraraudradbhuteshvatha
gandharasca nishadasca kartabau karuney rasey
dhaivatasca prajaktabyo bibhatsey sa bhayanakey

[The notes Madhyama and Pancama are to be produced in the Comic and the Erotic sentiments, Sadja and Rishabha in the Heroic, the Furious and the Marvellous sentiments, Gandhara and Nishada in the Pathetic sentiments, and Dhaivata is to be produced in the Odious and the Terrible sentiments]. Though the slokas (16 Ka—16 Kha) are placed below the slokas 13-14, (depicting the application of notes in a song as their corollary], the arrangements should rather have been vice-versa, because the principle underlying the basic theory about the exposition of sentiment from the svara is enunciated in the slokas cited earlier. The first sloka in the 29th chapter reads as :

sadjodicyabati caiba sadjamadhya tathaiba ca
madhyamapancamabahulyat karjyang sringarahasyayoh

The translation by Manomohan Ghosh follows : [The sadjadicyavati and the sadjamadhya should be applied in the

Erotic and the Comic sentiments respectively because madhyama and pancama are amplified in them]. That the songs were an intergal part of the drama and were applied to heighten its effect can easily be detected from the above sloka. Bharata details out in ten successive slokas all the jatis and their corresponding sentiments. Generally, the amsa notes are amplified. The respective sentiments that the jatis produce are :

Jatis belonging to Sadja grama			*Sentiments*
Sadjodicyavati	(M. P.)	Sringara, hasya	(Erotic, Comic)
Sadjamadhya	(M. P.)	,, ,,	(,, ,,)
Sadji	(S)	Vira, raudra, adbhuta	(Heroic, Furious, Marvellous)
Arsavi	(R)	,, ,, ,,	(,, ,, ,,)
Naisadi	(N)	Karuna	(Pathetic)
Sadjakaisiki	(G)	,,	(,,)
Dhaivati	(D)	Bibhatsa, bhayanaka	(Odious, Terrible)

[The letters within brackets are the notes for amplification.] Similarly, Bharata describes the sentiments expressed in the jatis in the madhyama grama.

The varnas are four as arohi, avarohi, sthayi, sancari. That the alamkaras depend on the varnas is narrated in the sloka

etan samasritan samyaglankarannibodhata

The alamkaras described in N.S., are thirty-three in number : Prasannadi, Prasannanta, Prasannadyanta, Prasannamadhya, Sama, Bindu, Venu, Nivritta-pravritta, Kampita, Kuhara, Recita, prenkholitaka, Mandrataraprasanna, Taramandraprasanna, Prasvara, Prasada, Udvahita, Avalokita, [Krama] Niskujita, Udgita, Hradamana, Ranjita, Avarta, Parivartaka, Udghathita, Akshipta, Sampradana, Hasita, Humkara, Sandhipracchadana, Vidhuna, Gatravarna. These depend on the four varnas[3] as under :

Sthayi	8	Alamkaras
Sancari	13	,,
Arohi	14	,,
Avarohi	5	,,

Among these Vidhuna (Arohi and Avarohi), Venu (Sancari and Avarohi), Prasannanta (Sthayi and Arohi), Prasannadi (Sthayi and Arohi), Recita (Sṭhayi, Sancari and Arohi), Sama (Sthayi and Sancari) alamkaras depend on more than one varna as shown within brackets. According to Bharata, when a regular song (pada) adds at least two varnas to it, then the varnas give rise to sentiments.

In another sloka Bharata refers to seven types or forms of songs as *saptarupagata* wherein these alamkaras are attached. But these songs are possibly quite old and traditional even in relation to the dhruvas. In a few slokas in chapter 31 (N.S.), these types are described in details. The discourse on alamkara ends with a brilliant poetic passage which reads as :

Sashina birahiteba nisha bijaleba nadi lata bipushpeba
abibhushiteba ca stri geetiralangkarahina syat

[A song without any alamkara will be like a night without the moon, a river without water, a creeper without a flower and a woman without any ornament].

The alamkaras are described by Bharata with much care and their relative difference effectively driven home. Among the thirty-three alamkaras only a few, such as Prasannadi, Prasannanta, Sama, Venu, Recita, Kampita, Prasvara, Prasada, Krama have a specific character. While Bharata stresses on the need for using alamkaras to the varnas, he has advised not to use too many of them. This reflects his keen sense and balanced judgement in aesthetic appreciation.

Bharata has dealt with, in the succeeding slokas, in this chapter, the various kinds of geetis, dhatus, vrittis, two kinds of veenas and the bahirgeetis. Geetis are of four kinds as Magadhi, Ardhamagadhi, Sambhavita and Prithula.

Prathama magadhi jneya dvitiya tvardhamagadhi
sambhavita tritya ca caturthi prithula smrita

The first one, Magadhi, is sung in different tempos ; the second, Ardhamagadhi, changes its tempo in the middle of the

6

song : the Sambhavita is constituted with long syllables while Prithula with short ones. But these geetis had no connection with the dhruvas ;

dhruvajogang binaiba hi

Rather, these are to be applied to the Gandharva only ;

Gandharva eba jojyastu nityang ganaprajokribhih

Dhatus relate to the actual mode of playing on the instruments and these are of four kinds : Vistara, Karana, Aviddha and Vyanjana. Even in modern times a musician might follow the above alamkaras while playing on his instrument with the least trouble. The process starts from expansion or amplification, leading to embellishments. The third stage is in breaking up the music, only to give it a final indication of its artistic unity. Bharata has mentioned all the ten varieties of Vyanjana giving detailed process of fingering and the strokes to be used. These are to be noted even to-day by the practical students of instrumental music.

The three Vrittis (gati-Vritti) are very important from the point of view of instrumental music. These relate mainly to the movement :

Tisro gatibrittayah pradhanyena grahjya citrabrittirdakshinasceti. Tasang vadyatalalayageetijatimargapradhanyani jathasvang vyanjanani bhabanti.

[Styles of procedure (gati Vritti) to be principally reckoned are three : Citra (Variegated), Britti (movement, i. e., having a simple movement) and Dakshina (dexterous). Instrumental music, time measure (tala), tempo (laya), geeti (Rhythm), yati and graha-marga (way of beginning)[4] will determine their respective characters]. It is not understood why Manomohan Ghosh translated rhythm for geeti !

Another class of jatis has been described which arises from the combination ot dhatus. Eventually, these are not the jatis described earlier as suddha and vikrita.

Then Bharata refers to the two kinds of veenas, which are citra and vipanci,

Saptatantri bhavetcitra bipanci nabatantrika
bipanci konabadya syatcitra cangulibadana.

Citra with seven strings was to be played with the fingers while vipanci, having nine strings, was played with the plectrum.

The thirtieth chapter, that on sushira, states a very important point regarding production of proper srutis from the flute. The sadja, madhyama and pancama, having four srutis, will arise from a hole (of the flute) fully open (vyakta-mukta) : dhaivata and rishabha, having three sruits each, will arise from a hole, played with shaken fingers (kampamana) ; while gandhara and nishada, with two srutis, from a hole partly free from the finger (ardhamukta). The music produced from the flute is steady, sweet and soothing when proper alamkaras are applied.

Bharata has stated the importance of tala almost at the end of Chapter 31, which he names as Talabidhanam or the Time-Measure. The sloka runs as under :

Jastu talang na janati na sa gata na badakah.

[One can not be a singer or a player of instruments unless one knows the tala.]
and there are three layas, as druta, madhya, vilambita that determines the tempo of tala. It should be remembered that the entire tala conception of Bharata was directly related to its application in the dhruva geetis, which were meant for drama (and accompanying dances). The definition of laya is to be conceived only under this background.

Bharata further says :

Chhandyoksharpadanang hi samatvang jatprakirtitam
Kalakalantarakritah sa layo manasangitah.

[That which is known as completion of metres, syllables and words, is called the laya or mana (measure) depending on the variation of timing in Kalas (in its tala)]

Manomohan Ghose has taken the word 'sama' here as equivalent to completion. The meaning perhaps would be more broad if we consider the word as balancing the three-fold aspects as metre, syllable and words into one unified scheme, which itself is the embodiment of laya.

Along with laya, one should also be careful about Jati and Pani. There are three Jatis as sama, srotagata aad gopuccha. "The Jati, when it has the same tempo in the beginning, in the middle and in the end,...............................is called Even (sama) ;...it predominates generally in the playing of instruments. The Jati which, in traversing the path of musical sounds, is sometimes staid and sometimes running, is called current-like (srotagata) generally used in songs". (Natyasastra Ch. 31, Sl. 490-93)

That the entire tala and laya scheme was primarily meant for dramatic songs and dances may further be corroborated from the slokas (Sl. 33-34) where Bharata mentions of the movement of hands and fingers. He also speaks of silent and audible talas.

The ancient unit for measurement of tala is nimesha 'time required for a twinkling of eyelids (footnote on p. 53, No. 3). There are different versions of the time-duration of nimesha, as 1 nimesha 1/11.25 second or 1/9 second and then 18 nimesha equivalent to 1 Kastha and 30 Kastha to 1 Kala ; and again, 5 nimeshas made one matra (which we should consider during songs and dances).

Apart from the significance of Kala as being related to the measurement of time, the word Kala has a specific significance in relation to tala, meaning the system of tala cycles which arises from grouping of matras.

The word tala, that refers to the beating of time by the clapping of hands [palm of the hands] is vitally related to Kala as it determines the character of laya. The pramana kala is said to correspond with the medium tempo while there are two more tempos, as drut and vilambita, recognised in musical performances. There are three kinds of kalas corresponding to three margas as citra, vritti and dakshina. In the citra, there should be three matras, in vritti twice of it, in dakshina, four times.

The tala is of two kinds, caturasra and tryasra having for their sources cancatputah and capapautah[5] respectively. These have four and three units of measurement, and consist of long and short syllables. It may be remembered that in ancient Hindu music hrasva, dirgha and pluta were considered as three successsive units of measurement of time in relation to matra, corresponding to one, two and three units respectively. Now, the cancatputah i. e., caturasra, consists of two long syllables, followed by one short and final pluta syllable ; whereas the capaputah i.e., tryasra consists of one long syllable followed by two short syllables and the final long syllable. The first one would have matras in multiple of 4, while the second, in multiple of 3.

And again, combination of these two varieties would result in mixed talas as shatpitaputrakah and pancapanih ; their subdivisions will again depend on varying arrangement of matras. The entire tala system, it may be seen, centres round these two broad divisions as caturasra and tryasra.

The thirtysecond chapter is exclusively devoted to dhruva geetis, their character, function, purpose, division and so on. But the greater half of it is full of illustrations of the metres used in different dhruvas. Bharata defines dhruva as

Vakyavarna jhyalankara laya jatyatha panayah
dhruvamanyonyasambandha jasmantasmad dhruva smrita.

[The dhruva is so called because in it words, varnas, alamakra, tempo, jati and panis are regularly (dhruvam) connected with one another.]

And what are those words and padas that constitute the dhruvas ? These are rik, panika, gatha and seven traditional types of songs. The dhruvas originate in various metres and are of five kinds, according to the requirement of the natyageeti, as pravesiki (entering), akshepiki (indicating), prasadiki (calming), antara (transitional) and naishkramiki (departing). Padas are composed of syllables and are of two kinds as nibadha and anibaddha, conforming again to two classes as a-tala and sa-tala. 'For the purpose of the dhruva, it must conform to a time-measure and is to be (regularly) composed !' The tala used in dhruva are tryasra and caturasra. In the dhruvas, padas should be regularly composed in strict pursuance of the syllabic metres.

Various metres are used according to types and sentiments of the dhruva geetis. The five classes of dhruvas have a number of limbs (anga) as mukha, pratimukha, sthita, pravritta, vajra, sandhi, samharana, prastara, upavarti, masaghata, caturasra, upapata, praveni, sirshaka, sampishtaka, antaharana and mahajanika.

Bharata then describes various metres with specific illustrations from dhruva geetis. These are dhriti and rajani, guru and sikha, malini, vithi, nalini and bhogavati, madhukarika and kusumavati or again, such metres as mudita and prakasita, vilambita or cancalagati. There are also application of traditional ancient metres as gayatri, anustup, brihati, jagati, udgata etc. Different metres are used according to the composition of syllables in the padas and again, according to the sentiment the pada conveys. Both the poetic and the emotive aspects are considered during the application of such metres. There are five formal aspects of dhruvas according to the application nf metres. These are jati, sthana, prakara, pramana, nama :

jati (h) *sthanang prakarasca pramanang nama caiba hi*

Bharata sets rigid rules for application of the dhruvas. While there are such specific metres, tala, laya etc., for pravesiki, akshepiki, prasadiki, antara and naishkramiki dhruvas, there is complete restriction also for its use at certain dramatic moments. 'Dhruvas should be thus applied after taking into consideration the rule regarding themes, places, times and seasons (involved), the characters (in the play) and indication of the states.

Bharata has directed wise men to apply the dhruvas after taking due consideration of the various aspects of the drama as theme, performance, characters, sentiments, psychological conditions etc. That he was conscious all the time of the aesthetic expression of these dramatic songs could well be ascertained from his method of analysis and details. Further, he had in his mind an image of symbolic representations while comparing gods, kings, men or women, the natural phenomena or the celestial being with appropriate counterparts.

There is suitable time also for these songs. When we come to know that pravesiki dhruvas are to be sung in the forenoon, we are immediately aware of such ragas that are demonstrated in the morning hours. Songs have been given by Bharata a primary status. Instrumental music and dance would follow songs. A performance is generally composed of these three, arranged in proper sequence, as mentioned.

And now the language of these geetis. Sanskrit songs are to be rendered when celestial beings are concerned ; in case of human beings, half-Sanskrit (near-Sanskritik language). Manomohan Ghose has pointed out that this reference to half-Sanskrit might be the earlier form of Sanskrit as a language. The major form of language to be used in the dhruva geetis are firstly Suraseni, secondly Magadhi. Suraseni is, however, the widely known language Sauraseni.

Time and again Bharata has made emphatic reference to the effect of songs within the drama proper. A drama does not attain its heightened aesthetic level without songs. He has drawn a beautiful comparison to justify his views. 'Dhruvas depending on the context and made to express sentiments suited to the situation, embellish the drama just as the stars illumine the sky'. He has further directed the sequence of these songs along with their corresponding gramas for proper rendition.

At the beginning, there should be songs in the madhyama grama followed by the one in the sadja grama. Next comes overlapping during the development, pancama in the pause and kaisika at the conclusion, in succession. The songs, in all four in kind as Magadhi, Ardhamagadhi, Sambhavita and Prithula, are to be sung in order. While padas are repeated in different tempos in the Magadhi, there would be just two repetitions in the Ardhamagadhi, and Sambhavita depending on heavy syllables ; Prithula, with lighter ones, is applied during instrumental music.

The last thirty-four slokas in this chapter have an abiding value which has not lost its significance since the time of Bharata even to this day. Both from the aesthetic as well as practical view of music, the observations of this great musicologist still holds good. He has defined, in these few slokas, what a song proper should be, what are the individual characteristics of a veena or a flute player, what are the qualities of a musical voice, and lastly, what are the faults of a singer. Let us take the description (how poetical) of a song :

Purnasvarang vadyabicitravarnang
tristhanasobhang trijatang trimatram
raktang samang slakshnamalang kritang ca
sukhaprajuktang madhurang ca ganam

[That which includes full notes, varnas, is embellished by instruments, relates to the three voice registers, has three Jatis and three matras, gives joy, is harmonious (sama) and delicate, contains alamkaras, is performed with ease, and has sweetness, is called a song per excellence].

Bharata has repeatedly stressed on the importance of such a song within the drama. Unless it is executed with proper care, he thinks, the drama stands a great risk in not being able to attain high standards. Music, in his opinion, is a fundamental component of drama.

By imparting philosophical insight into the nature of knowledge, Bharata describes how a musician should proceed to attain his or her objectives. He has referred to sweetness as well as softness of voice for all singers, they should have control over laya and tala, they should be of loving nature and of young age. The veena player should have nimble hands in producing sweet sounds and be supplemented with the qualities of good singers. The music of a flute should be steady, continuous expressive of varna and alamkara (The sloka 502 may be compared with the sloka 12 of chapter 30 of N.S.). The six qualities of voice, Bharata has referred as loud, compact, smooth, sweet, careful and distinctly related to three voice-registers. The faults have also been pointed out which are unsteady, bitten, nasal and so on. His practical sense as a musicologist would further be proved when we find that he has also analysed the qualities of a teacher and his disciple in two successive slokas.

The last chapter [i.e. 33] that Bharata deals with music is exclusively devoted to the covered instruments, avanaddha vadya. He describes their 'lakshmans' in details and speaks of the various classes as mridanga, panava and dardura. There is a legend about the creation of drums, i.e. pushkaras. The names of Svati and Narada are associated with the creation of these instruments. The legend thus runs : one day the sage Svati went to a nearby lake. There were torrential rains at that time. Indra wanted to make a great ocean out of this earth and so the rains did not stop. The rains were dropping at a great force on that lake. Supported with fierce winds on the leaves of the lotus of the lake, the rains produced distinctly audible sounds. The sage was at once attracted to it and discovered in the nature of that deep sound a rare beauty and wonder :

Jyesthamadhyakanisthang tu patranamabadharya ca
Gambhirang madhurang hridyamajagamasramang tatah

Manomohan Ghose has rendered the sloka as :

[After observing the high, medium and low sounds produced on the lotus-leaves as deep, sweet and pleasing, he (the sage Svati) went back to his hermitage.] A high sound in an instrument, whether it is stringed or covered, does not correspond with a 'deep' sound ; rather 'low' sound may be found to correspond with the 'deep' one. 'Medium' and 'low sounds' may both be sweet and pleasing at once. It would be better to take all these attributes mentioned by Bharata in the sloka as six different qualities.

After returning to his hermitage, Svati developed the various drums as mridanga, pushkara, panava and dardura with the help of Visvakarma. Dunduvi was an instrument played by the Gods. He made muraja as its counterpart, and then devised alingya, urdhvaka and arkika. He then covered the instruments with hide and bound them with strings.

The rendering by Manomohan Ghose of anga and pratyanga as major and minor 'limbs' does not perhaps carry proper sense (sl. 14). In an instrumental combine (Kutapavinyasa), the vipanci and citra [veenas] were of major importance whereas kacchapi [ektantri] and Ghosaka [tambura] were used as minor or supporting instruments. Under this background, the word 'limb' strikes unsound. Similarly, mridanga, dardura and panava were of major importance while jhallari and pataha were minor drums in the Kutapavinyasa. Flute had the characteristics of a major and the sankha and dakkini were of minor, or supporting instruments.

These instruments, Bharata urges, are to be played according to the sentiments prevailing in the drama. Moreover, in social life these instruments had a big role to play. In a festival or a royal procession, in marriage or birth ceremonies, or in battle all these are to be employed. Pushkara is a generalised term for covered instruments, the major three forms of which are mridanga, panava and dardura. These have again three main characteristics. Firstly, regular notes can be produced from these instruments. Secondly, various karanas might be formed. Thirdly, the instruments give rise to jatis. But the pushkara instruments have, in all, fiifteen specific characteristics as :

(1) 16 aksharas, (2) 4 margas, (3) vilepana, (4) 6 karanas, (5) 3 jatis ; (6) 3 layas; (7) 3 gatas ; (8) 3 pracaras ; (9)

3 samjogas , (10) 3 panis ; (11) 5 pani-prahata ; (12) 3 praharas ; (13) 3 marjanas ; (14) 18 jatis ; (15) 20 prakaras.

The sixteen aksharas are k, kh, g, gh, t, th, d [n], t, th, d, dh, [m], r, l, h. Of these, k, t, r, t, th, d, dh are to be produced on the right face ; g, h, and th on the left face of the drums ; th on the urdhavaka and k, r, n, dh, v and l on the alingya, [the akshara v is not, however, mentioned in the earlier list].

Further, aksharas are to be produced by combining vowels with these 16 consonants. The vowels are a, aa, i, ee, u, uu, e, ai, o, au, am, and ah. Bharata then goes on to describe in details the various combinations that are possible.

There are five kinds of hand strokes [paniprahata] as (1) samapani (level-handed) ; (2) ardhapani (half-handed) ; (3) ardharadhapani (quarter-face) ; (4) parsvapani (hand-side) ; and (5) pradesini (fore-finger).

The four margas are addita, alipta, vitasta and gomukha. These are to be derived by combining the various drums and their parts. A series of strokes of differing nature are to be found in each of these margas. These margas are to be applied according to different sentiments and the instruments are to be played in a dance to suit the proper sentiment and the state and gestures of the participating characters.

There are six karanas as (1) rupa ; (2) kritapratikrita ; (3) pratibheda ; (4) rupasesa ; (5) ogha ; (6) pratisuska. Karanas originate from playing of instruments. In ogha, known otherwise as catushka, all the instuments are played in slow tempo to produce sonant syllable.

The number of jati, laya and pani are three each. These are observed according to the liking of the performers. Druta, madhya and vilambita are the three tempos (laya) while sama srotogata and gopuccha are three jatis. Jati, laya and pani are interrelated and these are to be considered as a whole.

The three marjanas are mayuri, ardha-mayuri and karmaravi,

and are related to the notes of the puskaras. [The mayuri marjana will be in the madhyama grama, the ardha-mayuri in the sadja grama and the karmaravi in the gandhara grama, and these will include overlapping note].

Mayuri madhyamey gramey sadjey tvardha tathaiba ca
Karmaravi tu gandharey sadharanasamasrayah

Bharata has stressed on a very important point, that of achieving conformity while playing of drums. There are eight such conformities as, in syllables, limbs, tala, tempo, jati, graha, nyasapanyasa and pani. There were specific rules for playing of the drums in the dhruvas.

As in the case of musicians or instrument-players, Bharata has left his comments on the characteristics of a good drummer:

Gitavadyakalalayagrahamokshabisaradotha laghuhastah
Citrapanirbidhijna siddhisthaney dhruvakusalah
Kalabhiratah madhurahastah sunibishto
raktamarjanobalaban ;
Subihitasarirabuddhih sangsidhyo badakah sreshthah

[I shall next speak of the characteristics of a (good) player of drums. He who is an expert in songs, playing of instruments kala, tempo and who knows how to begin a song, to bring it to a finish, and has a nimble hand (in playing) and knows about the various panis, and (general) rules of the success, and is an expert in singing dhruvas, and who practises of kalas, and has a pleasing hand (in playing instruments), power of concentration, and who can produce pleasing marjana and is strong (in body), and regular in his physical and intellectual habits, and is an accomplished (artist), is called the best player (of drums)]. Bharata has also recorded the qualities of the mridanga, which would be able to produce distinct, clear, well-divided and controlled strokes. It should include the three marjanas and would be full of pleasing notes. He concludes his observations by saying that the playing of mridangas is the basis of the dramatic performance and play itself does not run any risk if the songs and the accompanying instruments are well produced.

Vadye ca geetey ca suprajuktey
natyaprayogey na bipattimeti.

1, Manomohan Ghosh, in his translation of N.S., has referred to the series (p. 7, Introduction) starting with SRGMPDN, which is not correct as could be seen in the sloka quoted above in respect of Madhyamagrama.

2 Manomohan Ghosh puts it as Arshabhi in place of Sadji, which seems quite correct. Moreover, Sadji and Gandhari make Sadjakaisiki.

3 The total alamkars come to 30 only. There is obviously a discrepancy of 3 more alamkars which has not been clarified.

4 Manomohan Ghose explains the Graha-marga as the manner of following a song or a piece of music by an instrument of tala. Under the context, it seems to be 'Sath Sangat' in modern practice.

5 Cancat putah and Capaputah are also termed as Caccatputah Cancuputah and cacaputah/Cayaputah respectively.

Brihaddesi

In between the period of Bharata and Sarangadeva, a span of more than one thousand years, Matanga seems to be the most significant musicologist whose contribution to the concept of music is still treated with reverence. More than one author as Matanga are found in sanskrit texts, while their existence as mortals spread over a few centuries. As from internal evidence, recorded in Brihaddesi we find the names of Jashtika and Durgasakti who lived in the beginning of the Christian era. Again, references to Matanga as a musician and a flute player are found in works dated 7th to 9th centuries. From all these evidences it may be surmised that Matanga, the author of Brihaddesi, wrote his treatise sometimes between the 5th and 7th centuries A. D.

K. Sambasiva Sastri, the editor of the Trivandrum edition (1928) of the book is rather sceptical about the date of composition of the MS., which was first exhibited from Travancore at the All India Conference of scholars and artists at Indore in 1921. Though the editor does not ascribe to it any date, yet he is sure of the 'merit' of this MS. and observes : "the treatise proposes to furnish new information on such subjects as the 'courses' of raga". The English rendering of the word 'course' for the sanskrit word marga is not, however, clear in the present context. In fact, Matanga himself described the chapter as entitled, ragalakshmanam. What the author has done here is to convey the idea of raga and the seven geetis as well as to record their characteristics with specific illustrations. The editor, however, quotes the most significant sloka that appears in the very first page of the treatise.

Desey desey prabrittasau dhvanirdesiti sanggitah

Matanga equates the term desi with dhvani. To him, dhvani is of supreme importance. But this dhvani, the manifestation of nada, has its root cause in bindu.

Tato bindustato nadastato matrastanukramat
Varnastu matrakodbhuta......

Matra originates from varna, varna from nada and nada from bindu. Everything then starts from that manifest particle. This philosophic attitude of the author is, perhaps, derived from his knowledge of the tantras.

His concept of dhvani is still wider. The entire world is manifested with dhvani as may be seen from the following slokas:

Dhvanirjonih para jneya dhvanih sarbasya karanam
akrantang dhvanina sarbang jagat sthabarajangamam

Here the word *akrantang* corresponds with manifestation ; the physical world itself is caused by dhvani which again is to be considered as the ultimate reality. This is surely a philosophic attitude per excellence towards the basic concept of music. Starting from this source knowledge he develops all his later findings. In the chapters on desi (dhvani), nada, sruti, svara, murcchana, tan, murcchana tan, varna, alamkara, geeta, jati, ragalakshmanam, bhasalakshman and prabandha, this development finds a systematic rendering with suitable illustrations of sargams wherever necessary.

Dhvani, Matanga gives here the traditional version, is of two kinds, vyakta and avyakta.

Dhvanistu dvibidhah prokto vyaktavyaktabibhagatah

The song, that is derived from dhvani, should be sung with much feeling,

geeyatey sanuragena

and that marga geeti is both nibaddha and anibaddha.

The chapter on nada is important as it expounds Matanga's philosophic attitude in specific terms :

Na nadena bina gitam na nadena bina svarah

and again,

Nadarupaih smrito Brahma nadarupo Janardana
nadarupa para saktirnadarupo Mahesvarah.

Matanga has almost identified nada with the param Brahma. He has also spoken of the brahmagranthi sthana, where

Tanmadhye sangsthitah pranapranad bahnisamudbhabah
bahnimarutasanjogannadah samupajayatey

Sarangadeva, in his famous treatise, Sangitratnakara, has spoken of this brahmagranthi in the very first sloka of Svaragatadhyaya. Continuing further, Matanga has narrated five stages through which nada develops and manifests itself :

Sukshmascaibatisukshmasca vyaktovyaktasca kritrimah

[sukshma, atisukshma, vyakta, avyakta and krittrima]. Sambasiva Sastri has referred to the words as nibandha and anibandha. But the MS. reading is probably correct. Svami Prajnanananda has inferred that Kohala and others were also responsible, before Matanga, for such philosophic interpretation of nada and dhvani[1]. The final stage i.e. Kritrima is the manifested one. Kohalacharya has mentioned of 'individual will' *(atmochhya)* as the cause of dhvani.

Matanga has given a very generalised description of sruti as

Sruyanta iti srutayah

In this chapter he has referred to many other musicologists as Bisvabasu, Bharata, Kohala and Catura (?) and focussed their opinion. But Matanga has given a fine explanation as to the nature of sruti :

...sopanapadakramena

Sruti is one and absolute, but it rises from its original point higher and higher as along a staircase. As for other attributes he has accepted traditional opinion. That a particular svara may have two, three or four srutis, or that the total number of srutis are twenty-two are all accepted versions. He has also referred to two similar veenas for determining the position of srutis. This was elaborately dealt with in Natyasasrta by Bharata Muni. In two very poetic descriptions he has conceived of ananta sruti. Relative sruti positions in the two gramas as sadja and madhyama grama have been detailed out with two diagrams. The entire gamut he has referred to as *srutimandalam*. Matanga has thereby made his conceptual understanding about sruti and the octave or the grama quite clear and convincing.

Matanga has given two definitions of the term svara, which are both significant for its clarity. Firstly, he says,

Svayang jo rajatey jasmad tasmadesha svarah smritah

The svara is self-existent, is derived from its very essence. Secondly, he connects the meaning of the word svara with raga :

Ragajana (ko) dhvanih svara iti

A raga is manifested through the svaras. He then describes the qualities of svara which is one and varied at the same time, it is all pervasive and permanent, it is ultimately indestructible.

Nityoabinasi Vyapakah sarbagatah

This is both a scientific and philosophic postulate at the same time.

The vadi, samvadi, anuvadi and vivadi svaras are but the king, his minister, attendants and enemy respectively. But the function of the vadi svara lies in its achieving the essential quality of a raga :

Ragasya ragatvang janayati

This is a very sound argument. Instead of a superficial treatment, Matanga has defined the vadi svara in a way as to reflect its inner quality.

In determining the jati, kula, varna and devata (deity) of the svaras, Matanga has adopted the conventional view. While the colour of sadja is like the petal of a lotus, that of nishada conjures up all the colours at a time. The two slokas describing the different colours of the svaras are highly poetic and attain an artistic and imaginative beauty.

The distribution of rasa or sentiment in each svara is as follows :

S, R —Vira, raudra and adbhuta ;
G —Karuna ;
M —Hasya ;
P —Sringara ;
D —Bibhatsa, bhayanaka ;
N —Karuna.

The sentiment evoked by G and N is the same ; it may also be noted that G and N stands with each other in vadi-samvadi relation i. e. N is at the thirteenth sruti from G.

The position of the human body wherefrom the svara originates has been determined as :

S —Kantha (Mouth)
R —Sira (Head)
G —Nasika (Nose)
M —Ura (Heart)
P —Ura, Sira, Kantha (Heart, Head, Mouth)
D —Talu (Palate)
N —All the positions combined together.

For the discussion of grama, Matanga has not ascribed separate headlines, possibly because, he has taken the svaras as the principal ingredients out of which the concept of grama has arisen as their subsidiary. Only in a few slokas Matanga has dealt with this intricate topic, though with great lucidity :

Samuhabacinau gramau svarasrutyadisanjutau
jatha kutumbinah sarba ekibhutva basanti hi

Svami Prajnanananda has given a very suitable explanation of Matanga's concept of grama. Svaras are basically responsible for the outline of a raga, and grama is that closed periphery within which the raga moves and develops itself.[2] Matanga has also given a nice picture of the grama where all the near relatives of different families live in unity with perfect understanding amongst themselves. The musical scale or grama is also like a village where all the svaras develop to form a raga achieving the right melodic pattern. Only two gramas were in existence, that of sadja and madhyama. He quotes Narada's view that Gandhar grama was never in use on this earth. The svaras were originated from samaveda and grama was made possible because of the existence of these svaras. And what was the real function of a grama ! Matanga answers to this as follows :

Svarasrutimurchanatanajatiraganang vyabasthapanatvang nama prayojanam

Svara, sruti, murchana, tan, jati and raga all these are to be encompassed and synchronised into one complete whole and this is possible because of the existence of a grama.

Matanga, it may be seen, has tried to define the attributes from their etymological significance. Murchana means cadence. The sequence of notes that helps a raga to produce the proper cadence is a murcchana :

Murchatey (?) *jena rago hi murchanetyabhisanggita*

Murchana is of two types, one composed of seven notes, the other composed of twelve notes. The second variety of murchana has earlier been recorded by Nandikesvara ; Matanga also admits it in a sloka. Of the former variety, there are four classes as purna, sharaba, ouduvita, sadharana, according to the use of number of svaras. While the first three classes comprise of seven, six and five notes respectively, the sadharana class comprises of the kakali and antara svaras. But the most significant aspect of Matanga's discussion on the chapter on murchana lies in his comparative assessment of murchana and tan. Matanga answers to his self-styled question :

Nanu murchanatanayo ko bhedah. Ucyatey...murchanarohakramena tanoabarohakramena bhabatiti bhedah.

Murchana is the sequence of svaras in the ascending order, while tan is in the descending order. Matanga has thereafter given examples of varieties of tans of seven, six, five notes and so on. There should be two methods of the application of tans. He has quoted here Bharata's observations :

Dvibidha tanakirya tantryah prabesanang nigrahastatha

These are introductory and concluding tans. The word nigraha has different meanings. But it should be taken for 'to restrain or conclude' in this context. Matanga then gives specific examples of kuta tans, four varnas as sthayi, sancari, arohi and abarohi, and emphasizes that a song is nothing but *varnasabda.* Matanga mentions of the alamkars which do, of course, resemble with those mentioned by Bharata in his Natyasastra. He has described those alamkars with concrete examples.

In the chapter on geeti he has, of course, nothing new to add except the four forms of traditional geetis. He has ascribed respective marga, tala and matra to each kind of geeti. The succeeding two chapters on jati and ragalakshmanam are dealt with quite exhaustively. Here Matanga has said something which is not very original indeed, but reflects perfectly well his method of independent analysis.

He has spoken of eighteen jatis in all, seven in the sadja grama and eleven in the madhyama grama. Then he has mentioned the general and specific characteristics of the jatis. Apart from the existence of the formal aspects as sruti, graha svara etc., he stresses on the evocation of rasa 'as an important manifestation of jati. The ten lakshmanas are those already stated by Bharata,

Jasmadjjayatey rasapratitirarabhyata iti jatayah (jatah ?)

But the point where he differs from Bharata is genuinely interesting. Bharata has taken graha and amsa svara as identical, but Matanga has been specific in his description of the amsa svara :

Jasminnangsey kriyamaney ragabhivyakti rbhabati (bhih) syoamsa

Amsa is that svara which determines or exposes the character of a raga.

And then what is a raga ? What are its characteristics, asks Matanga. He himself answers in the following sloka :

Ranjako janacittanang sa ca raga udahritah

There is, of course, nothing exceptional in his exposition. But he has mentioned of seven geetis (different from those four geetis as magadhi etc.) which may be generally termed as raga geeti, having their composition based on melody types. These are suddha, bhinnaka, godika, raga geeti, sadharani, bhasha geeti, bibhasha. Matanga has, however, elaborately exemplified the important ragalakshmanas with reference to particular ragas. Here is a typical example :

Sadjangsau pancamo nyasah Kaisikijatisambhavah
tatha karmarabhijateh svaraih purnaisca kaisikah

There is another important observation by Matanga. Grama

raga has given rise to bhasha ; bhasha has, in turn, given rise to bibhashika (bibhasha) and lastly, antarabhasha has sprung out from bibhasha. This sequence is of much importance in order to trace out the development of the raga system.

In the last chapter Matanga describes the prabandha gana. He has mentioned of such varieties britta, dandaka, varnaka, kaibada, pratapabardhana etc. A prabandha is composed in Karnata bhasha having such limbs as tala, pata, viruda etc. The various forms are also described in details.

It appears, there was also a chapter on vadya, as referred to in sl. 511. But that has not been discovered as yet. The earlier musicologists, whose names he has mentioned with reverence to substantiate his views, are Brahma, Narada, Bharata, Mahesvara, Kasyapa, Sardula, Kohala, Dattila, Nandikesvara, Ballava, Bisvabasu, Jastika, Durgasakti.

1. Svami Prajnanananda : Sangit O Samskriti
2. ,, : ibid

Sangitratnakara

Considered to be the most ambitious work on Indian music, Sangitratnakara by Sarangadeva has been recognised by scholars as a quite authoritative and comprehensive discourse on the subject yet attempted by any other musicologist.

In discussing the orgin of music and its structural development leading to the formation of raga system elaborating as well the major forms of music prevalent during his time, Sarangadeva has meticulously tried to explore the historical and the aesthetic aspects of Indian music. He had to take, therefore, a broad liberal view most of the time. The slokas, sometimes verging on philosophy and rhetoric, give a detailed analysis of the existing system of musical forms, which are, by no means, clear to us even to-day. The author himself has admitted, in slokas 20 and 21 of the Svargatadhyaya (padarthasangraha), that his work is based on the writings of other great musicologists who lived before his time. But that does not rob the book of its individual merit.

Sarangadeva gives a brief introduction about himself as was the prevailing custom with the authors. One of his forefathers, Bhaskara, hailing descent from the sage Vrisagana of Kashmir, settled in the South ; Sodhala, son of Bhaskara, and the father of Sarangadeva, lived under the patronage of king Singhana of the Yadava dynasty, who ruled Debgiri from 1210 to 1247 A. D. Sarangadeva was in service of King Singhana.

No less important are the two commentaries[1] of Kallinatha and Simhabhupala which throw much light on the original work. Simhabhupala, the earlier commentator, belonged to the Richerla dynasty and had a small kingdom. Though born of a low caste, he imbibed the best cultural tradition and had the temperament of a scholar, spending much of his time in the studies of alamkara [Rasarnavasudhakara, ascribed to him, was published in 1916 A. D.]. Kallinatha's grandfather was Vallabhadeva who lived in the city Vidyanagari, ruled by King Devaraya. His parents were Laksmidhara and Narayani. Kallinatha wrote this commentary on the advice of King Immadi Devaraya. There are a few more commentaries on this great work.[2]

The plan of the book is exhaustive and he has dealt, in the seven broad chapters, with the (1) Svara (2) Raga (3) Prakirnaka (4) Prabandha (5) Tala (6) Vadya (7) Nritta (Nritya ?). Of course, most of the ancient texts were modelled on the same pattern. Nritta was then considered as an integral part of music and most of the theoreticians dwelt on this aspect in details.

The opening slokas of the Sangitratnakara suggest the divine association of music. The philosophical aspect of Indian music has been a subject of great interest with all the musicologists. In fact, music has been studied with the same amount of religious devotion as religion itself was being studied.

C. Kunhan Raja has quite appropriately made this suggestive statement in the introduction to the Sangitratnakara, "The musical notes are the physical manifestations of the Highest Reality termed Nada-Brahman. Music is not a mere accompaniment in religious worship ; it is religious worship itself,..."

These few lines will explain how Indian music expresses the most intimate realization of man and how it helps the musician, in the process, to be aware of the Ultimate Reality. About the purpose of writing this treatise the author considers his attempt as an exploration of the eternal truth and religion through music (Sl. 14 p. 11). The music, further, satisfies the Gods, Lord Brahma is himself fond of samaganas, Goddess Sarasvati has also her own veena. And finally, man can attain all his material and spiritual desires through music.

Giten priyate deba ...
Samageetirato Brahma veenaasakta Sarasvati
Kimanye jakshagandharvadevadanavamanavah
... ...
dharmarthakamamokshanamidamebaikasadhanam

Kallinatha, in his commentary, quotes the famous sloka of Jajnabalkya :

Veenabadanatatvaggah srutijatibisaradah
talaggaschaprayasena mokshamargang sa gachati

It may seem, at a first glance, rather superfluous the long narratives describing the anatomy and physiology of the human body, the *brahmagranthi*, the nadis and so on. But a comprehensive view of musicology needs such elaboration when the production of svara, the manifestation of nada, is considered fundamentally a physiological factor. It is also curious to note that there has been an infusion of the *tantric* cult in this delineation. It may be remembered that during the centuries preceding the compilation of this treatise, people witnessed a great tantric movement in some parts of India.

Svaragatadhyaya has been spread out in eight subdivisions consisting of general definition of sangeeta, the description of human body, nada, sruti, svara, grama, murchana tana, sadharanalamkara, jati and geeti.

Sarangadeva begins his work by praising Lord Sankara, the embodiment of nada :

Brahmagranthijamarutanugatina cittena hritpankajay
surinamanuranjaka srutipadang joang svayang rajatey,
jasmad gramabibhagavarnaracanalamkarajatikramo
bandey nadatanung tamuddhurajagatgitang mudey Sankaram.

[I worship for happiness that Sankara, the embodiment of sound, sung about by the entire world, who shines by himself in the heart-lotus of the wise, giving delight to their ears through the mind that follows the breath arising out of the Brahmagranthi, and from whom villages, wealth, caste, the creations, ornaments, etc. arise]. Here perhaps the translator has oversimplified the proper meaning of the word 'grama' which he has rendered as village. Grama is a musical term meaning the cycle of svaras from sadja to nishada. Sarangadeva has explained the word in the first sloka of Chapter 4 of Svaragatadhyaya. The author has given a comprehensive list of musicologists who existed before his time and has acknowledged his indebtedness to them. Some of them are Sadasiva, Siva, Brahma, Bharata, Kasyapa, Matanga, Jashtika, Kohala, Dattila, Nanyabhupala etc. He has also named some of the leading alamkariks as Rudrata, Lollata, Abhinabagupta etc. He has not, however, mentioned of Anandavardhana, the great Kashmiri rhetorician, nor has he referred to Locana Kavi[3] the author of Ragtarangini, who existed during the reign of Ballalasena in Bengal. Sarangadeva has himself admitted that he has collected his material from the writings of these musicologists to prepare his treatise on music, which he describes as geeta, vadya and nritta (and not nritya ?) taken together :

Geetang badyang tatha nrittang trayang sangitamucyatey

Next he describes the two kinds of music, marga and desi. About the marga type of music, there is a great deal of confusion amongst the musicians even to-day. This has been loosely associated with the raga tradition of Indian music. There are, it seems, three possible ways of explaining the marga type of music. Sarangadeva himself gives one explanation :

Margo desiti tad dvedha tatra margah sa ucyatey
Jo margito birincadaih prajukto Bharatadivih
debasya purato sambhorniyatabhyudayapradah
desey desey jananang jaducya hridayaranjakam
geetang ca badanang nrittang taddesityabhidiyatey

[That (music) is of two kinds, Marga and Desi. Of these, that ia called Marga, which being sought for by the creator and others (and) performed by Bharata and others in front of God Siva, is invariably the producer of beatitude. That which, according to taste, gives delight to the hearts of people in different regions are (what is) called Desi.] Matanga has stated almost the same thing in his definition of desi in Brihaddesi.

Desey desey prabrittosau dhvanirdesiti sanggitah

Sarangadeva has associated marga music with Divinity. Secondly, if we take into account the etymological significance of the word marga, we can perhaps get at a near corollary. It is that type of geeti, practised by the gandharvas, which led them along the true path to the God. A third significance of this type of music may be had from its association with the marga tala that might have existed in ancient music. It had been a custom to render songs in the Citra, Vritti (Vartik) and Dakshina marga. The songs thus rendered were used to be called marga geeti. Equally fallacious would be to equate the 'desi ganam' with the regional or folk tunes of India. Sarangadeva has emphasized on the particular aesthetic quality of these songs.[4] The fact whether these songs had a pattern, or based on rigid system, is not clarified. But it may be stated, taken all the views together, that desi was a generalised term for all true music which had the sublime quality of satisfying the aesthetic taste of the listeners and had a deep-rooted base in the prevailing music systems of the country.

Among the three items that constitute music proper singing has been given the prime place. Next in importance comes instrument, then dancing. But for all practical purposes, it seems, these three forms of art were so well-knit, and their expressions so depending on one another that the question of introducing such points does not arise in the context. The author admits of seven suddha svaras and twelve vikrita ones while detailing his plan for the seven adhyayas comprising this treatise. He gives a short outline of each adhyaya outlining the specific subjects he is going to deal with. In the seventh adhyaya when he treats dancing, he has given due emphasis on the rasa aspect. It may be remembered that while he had previously referred to the musicologists, he did acknowledge his indebtedness also to the rhetoricians, He has not treated music just on its technical merit. He has in mind that poetry, aesthetics, philosophy and religion are all component parts of this art and a systematic study and practice of these aspects can only lead to its total comprehension.

After a brief reference to the nada, Sarangadeva has exhaustively dealt with the physiology, vital functions of prana and anala, – the process has ultimately led to a minute analysis of the body-structure. But, in doing so, he has raised certain philosophical enquiries as to the nature of the Brahmana :

Nirbikarang nirakarang sarvesvaramanasvaram
sarvasakti ca sarvaggang tadangsa jibasanggaka

And what is Brahmana ? Akasa has been created out of atmana, vayu from akasa, and then anala, jala, thence prithivi. These are the mahabhutas, the aggregate or sum total of the Brahmana. Human life is but a particle of that Sarvasakti, but being an integral part of the Brahmana, human soul is also capable of realizing the essence of ultimate truth. The Brahmana is *cidananda* and so is human being. The divine qualities have also been attributed to him. This particular human body is the receptacle of the nada, which is of two kinds, ahata and anahata. From this nada, varna is evoked and from varna, the pada, which is responsible for the song.

The power of the Brahmana resides in the *kundalini* of the human body, which, when raised, gives the true enjoyment, *jogananda* :

Asti kundalini brahmasaktiradharapankajey

The self, becoming conscious and active along with on the *kundalini*, is capable of obtaining perpetual bliss from music, but this music can be achieved only through the ahata nada. The song contemplates on the anahata, while human beings are used to the production of ahata nada, that creates the entire music through the medium of sruti. This music is not only pleasing, but also eradicates worldly misery. So this music is lokaranjanam, and bhabaranjanam at the same time.

The concept of nada has been equated with the idea of Brahmana and as such, musicologists have termed this word as nada-brahma. Sarangadeva speaks of it as an all-pervading consciousness, with the powers of Divinity. So he worships the nada-brahma before describing Him. The nada is evoked in the following way :

Jatah pranagnisanjogattena

We may compare the slokas of Matanga in this context

Bahnimarutasanjogannadah samupajayate

Nada is produced by the conjunction of prana (vayu) and anala (agni). There are, in all, five kinds of nada as atisukhsma, sukshma, pushta, apushta, kritrima. It may be described, however, as five stages of the same nada as will be evident from the sloka which states that these kinds emanate from five different places of the body in sequence :

pancasthanasthita kramat

Matanga here again has definitely stated the five positions in the body from which these sounds emanate. But Matanga has referred to vyakta and avyakta against pushta and apushta, as stated by Sarangadeva. Simhabhupala has explicitly pointed out this difference by quoting the entire sloka from Brihaddesi. On an ultimate analysis and for all practical purposes, there are three positions in the body from which the nada emanates, the heart, the throat and the head (Hridi, Kantha and Sira or murdha respectively) and these positions are termed as mandra, madhya and tara in relation to the twenty-two srutis. These positions are situated at a distance, twice to each other. For example, the sadja note in the tara position has twice the frequency of the sadja note of the madhya when struck in the wire of a veena and again the frequency in the sadja note of the madhya is double that of the mandra position.

Sarangadeva next describes sruti, which forms the most interesting as well as a highly intriguing subject to a musicologist. The relation between sruti and grama on the one hand and that of sruti and svara on the other are two vital discussions in the history of raga music of India. Consequently, all the theoreticians have laid strong emphasis on the proper understanding of the subject. There are twenty-two srutis in all placed at equal and indivisible distance to each other ; [according to modern physics this equality in division—as denoted by vibration frequency per sec.—does not hold good]. In order to prove that these srutis are at an equal distance the method of shifting the srutis of the *chala* veena with that of the corresponding *achala* veena was prescribed by the ancient musicians. The method which is better known as *sarana* has been elaborately described by Sarangadeva[5]. There are such four stages that lead to the establishment of the fact that there is no interval between two srutis and that the distance between the two successive srutis is equal. The srutis can only be discerned by hearing i.e. sravana (listening intensely) and so these dhvanis are termed srutis

Srabanchhrutayo

The srutis have gone in the ascending order with a regular system

Uchchochataratajukta

Bharata has also described the process in his Natyasastra.

Referring to the character and qualities of the svara that is derived from the sruti Sarangadeva states :

......jah snigdho anuranantmaka

Svato ranjayati srotricittang sa svara ucyatey

[What is soft, what is of the form of resonance, what gives aesthetic joy to the mind of the hearer, that is called a Svara].

Visvabasu, an ancient musicologist, refers to sruti as that sound which is discernible to the listener :

srabanendriyagrajhyatvad dhvanireba srutirbhavet

From these two definitions of svara and sruti the relation of sruti to svara may be established,—rather it may be said that sruti is responsible for the origin of svara.

Kohala, another musicologist referred to by Sarangadeva, gives a rhetorical description of sruti, that is highly poetical in context :

anantyang hi srutinang ca sucayanti bipascita
jatha dhavanibiseshanamanantyang gaganodarey
uttalapabanodbelajalarasisamudbhava
iattang pratipadyantey na tarangaparampara

Srutis are innumerable in number—in the expanse of the limitless sky—just like the countless drifting waves resulting from the lusty winds dashing against the sea.

The 16th and 17th slokas in the sixth part of the 1st prapathaka in Naradiyasiksha contain a lively description of the organic relationship between sruti and svara.

As to the nature of sruti Parsvadeva, another musicologist, has stated in his work Sangitsamayasara that the srutis are but twenty-two nadas. It is difficult to express these srutis through voice, these can properly be manifested only through the veena. Parsvadeva clearly states that the srutis are so delicate and the tonal difference between a particular sruti to its next higher or lower one is so small that human voice is not capable enough to express such srutis accurately.

The distinction between svara and sruti is to be summed up in the following manner : Sruti is just any sound caused due to immediate striking a string strung at a certain pitch, but the svara is that sound culminating in the resonance due to the series of sounds in the same pitch as an effect of the striking of that string. So, the source of both sruti and svara is the same. Srutis are of five varieties as Dipta, Ayata, Karuna, Mridu, Madhya.

Deepta ayata ca karuna mridurmadhyetijatayah

The twenty-two srutis are distributed among these five kinds of sruti. Dr. C. Kunhan Raja, who has translated the Svaragatadhyaya has given a chart showing the distribution as :

Dipta	Sa	Tivra	(Fierce)
(illuminated)	Ga	Raudri	(Terrible)
	Ma	Vajrika	(Thunderbolt)
	Ni	Ugra	(Mighty)

Ayata	Sa	Kumudvati	(Lily-pond)
(extended)	Ga	Krodha	(Wrathful)
	Ma	Prasarini	(Spreading)
	Pa	Sandipani	(Shining)
	Dha	Rohini	(Ascending)
Mridu	Sa	Manda	(Slow)
(soft)	Ri (Re)	Ratika	(Loving) (Raktika ?)
	Ma	Priti	(Happiness)
	Pa	Kshiti	(Earth)
Madhya	Sa	Chandovati	(Metrical)
(medium)	Ri	Ranjani	(Pleasing)
	Ma	Marjani	(Cleaning)
	Pa	Rakta	(Beloved)
	Dha	Ramya	(Charming)
	Ni	Kshobhini	(Agitating)
Karuna	Ri	Dayavati	(Merciful)
(mercy)	Pa	Alapini	(Singing)
	Dha	Madanti	(Intoxicating)

The translator comments on the above chart as :

"All the names have some meaning : but they are purely arbitrary and as such the meanings have no application here. But the matter deserves careful consideration whether the terms like Mridu denotes the quality like the interval or ratio with the previous svara. All the terms denote a quality of the svara except one, namely Karuna. Does it mean extremely soft, in relation to Mridu ? Whether the terms are arbitrary or are significant must be considered in detail". It may be seen from the chart that the :

1st, 8th, 10th, and 21st	Srutis	encompass	Dipta
2nd, 9th, 11th and 19th	"	"	Ayata
3rd, 7th, 12th and 14th	"	"	Mridu
4th, 6th, 13th, 15th 20th, and 22nd	"	"	Madhya
5th, 17th and 18th	"	"	Karuna

It is true that all the names bear aesthetic response and certain emotional attributes, but as C. Kunhan Raja points out, their relative significance are yet to be established. The second chart also does not reveal any method, except that Dipta, Ayata etc. have taken successively the 1st, 2nd...srutis.

For practical purposes of singing, the twenty-two srutis are modified in the form of twelve svaras (notes) and these are three-fold according to their diffrences in position called Mandra, Madhya and Tara. Madhya Sa is twice the Mandra Sa and Tara Sa is twice the Madhya Sa. This can be mathematically established as the relative vibrations per second of these notes are 256, 512 and 1024 (when a stringed wire is made to produce sound). But that the svaras are at equal intervals having uniform progression can not be proved in arithmetical terms, though the placing of the strings of *chala* veena with that of *achala* veena at equal intervals has been an accepted fact with the ancient musicologists.

There are a few intriguing terms relating to sruti positions of the notes Sa, Ga and Ni. The terms sadharana, antara and kakali are related correspondingly to these notes referred to earlier :

cyuto acyuto dvidha sadjo dvisrutirbikrito bhavet
sadharaney kakalitvey nishadasya ca drisyatey

[Sadja as modified is of two kinds, fallen and unfallen, with two srutis. It is seen (thus) in the case of Sadharana and of Kakalitva of Nishada.]

Dr. C. Kunhan Raja explains later that 'Sadja as suddha is in the fourth sruti. When Sa is placed on the third sruti and Ri starts from the fourth, instead from the fifth, and when Sa starts only from the 2nd instead of the first sruti, it is called the Sadharanatva of Sa. When...Sa starts only from the third sruti, Ni taking the first two srutis, that is called the case of Kakalitva of Ni' ; and again referring to Ga, Dr. Raja points out : Ga has only two srutis. Where Ga is fixed at 11 instead of at 9 and Ma is fixed at its natural sruti of 13, then also Ma has only two srutis (12 and 13) and Ga has four srutis (8, 9, 10 and 11). This is the case of Antaratva of Ga'. This has been clearly explained in the next chapter :

Srutidvayang cyetsadjasya nishada sangsrayettada
sa kakali madhyamasya gandharastvantara svarah

[Nishada takes over two srutis of Sadja, then that Svara is Kakali, but if Gandhara (so takes the two srutis) of Madhyama, (that Svara) is Antara].

The positions of the notes SRGMPDN are at the 4th, 7th, 9th, 13th, 17th, 20th and 22nd srutis respectively and whenever a particular note is displaced from its original sruti position, two notes change their relative position. This emphasis on cyuta notes has lost its significance in the context of modern classical music when fixed Komal and Kari notes have come into standard usage. For musicians such notes as atikomal, komal and anukomal terms have also come into existence thereby calssifying all the twenty-two srutis within a standard scale. The main[6] notes are correspondingly produced by such birds and animals as the peacock, cataka, ram, krauncha, cuckoo, frog and the elephant. The association of the note pancama with the voice of cuckoo is an old and traditional one, but the entire theory depends on the fixed tonic produced by the peacock and its relation with the consecutive notes as produced by other birds and animals. Whether they conform to accurate sruti positions is a matter yet to be experimented upon, but the nature and the tonal quality of sounds of the birds and animals are almost the same as are produced at those particular svaras. The ascending order of the svaras from S to N has, however, a scientific basis which relates more to psychology and physiology than that to mere conjecture. This is a matter for more detailed analysis.

Sarangadeva then states a very important proposition, that of the vadi samvadi etc. and its mutual relation :

Caturbidha svara vadi samvadi ca vivadyapi
anuvadi ca vadi tu prayogey bahulah svarah

srutayo dvadashsntau ba jajorantaragocharah
mithah sangvadinau tau.

[Svaras are of four kinds, namely Vadi and Samvadi, and also Vivadi and Anuvadis, but in performance, Vadi is the frequent svara. If between two (svaras) there is scope for an interval of twelve or eight srutis, they are mutually Samvadis].

Simhabhupala, in his commentary, has referred to Matanga and Dattila who have tried to establish a difference of 13 srutis instead of 12 regarding vadi and samvadi relations. The commentator has also analysed the vadi-samvadi relations of the notes in both the sadjagrama and madhyamagrama.

Sarangadeva then treats of the jati, kula and origin of the notes. These are based on mythology and have little connection either with scientific or philosophical understanding. There are also seven specific metres (chandas) for the seven notes, these are : Auushtup, Gayatri, Trishtup, Brihati, Pangkti, Ushnik and Jagati. As to the application of the notes he has pointed out specific rasas :

Sari birey adbhutey raudrey dhi bibhatsey bhayanakey
karjau gani tu hasyasringarayormapau

[Sa and Ri must be used in Vira, Adbhuta (and) Raudra : Dha in Bibhatsa and Bhayanaka ; Ga and Ni in Karuna ; Madhyama and Pancama in Hasya and Sringara.]

Can it follow then that the ragas with respective notes as vadi will reflect the particular rasa expressive of that note, for example, Iman Kalyan will express Karuna (Ga is vadi here) and Malkaus will express Hasya and Sringara (Ma is vadi here) ? Or, the process of equating a note with a particular rasa has its origin in the natyasangita before and during the time of Bharata ? (Bharata himself has instructed the musicians to sing songs according to the prevailing sentiment of the scenes being enacted on the stage).

The fourth sub-chapter of the Svaragatadhyaya is perhaps the most important if we consider the practical aspect of ancient music prevalent before the time of Sarangadeva. It deals with the concept of grama, formation of murchana, krama and tana. The word grama literally means a village populated by a group of persons more or less with a common language, custom, habit and religion and they are socially bound together in an atmosphere of kinship. It is this analogy of these people inhabiting a village that has attracted the notice of the musicologists to compare the svaras, murchana etc. that are bound together to a broad framework that may be termed grama. Perhaps no other musicologist has stressed more accurately on the concept of grama than Matanga. This has been referred to in a previous chapter where Brihaddesi has been dealt with at length. Sarangadeva has defined the grama in the simplest way possible, which, to the interested readers, might need further clarification. Both the commentators, Kallinatha and Simhabhupala, have exhaustively dealt with the subject. Sarangadeva says :

Gramah svarasamuhah syanmurchanadeh samasrayah
tau dvau dharataley tatra syatshadjagrama adimah
dvitiya madhyamagramah

[Grama is the collection of svaras, which form the basis for the Murchana etc. Two of them exist in this world. There the first is sadja grama. The second is Madhyama Grama.]

There was the third grama, gandhara grama that was obsolete on earth, but current in the Heaven, according to the ancients. But, of these three gramas, even the madhyama grama went out of practice after the time of Sarangadeva. Kallinatha has tried to explain the concept of grama in the following manner :

jatha lokey janasamuho grama ityucyatey, ebamatra
svarasamuho grama iti bibakshitah.

As people speaks of a grama (village) as inhabited by people so is a grama composed of the various svaras. Simhabhupala has quoted the sloka of Parsvadeva from his Sangitsamayasara :

Svaranang murchanatanajatijatyang sakatmanam
byabasthitasrutinang hi samuho grama ishyatey

Grama is composed of svaras, murchana, tana, jati, amsa and sruti and all these arranged in a definite order.

These three gramas differed in respect of their sruti positions. In the sadja grama, pancama is placed on its 4th sruti, while in the madhyama grama pancama is placed on its 3rd sruti, dhavita being placed automatically on its 4th sruti. The sruti relations as to the other svaras in those two gramas have remained fixed, while those in the gandhara grama is somewhat different from both the sadja and madhyama gramas ; pancama is, however, placed on the 3rd sruti, as in madhyama grama. A clear picture may be found from the following chart :

	S	R	G	M	P	D	N
Sadja grama	4	3	2	4	4	3	2
Madhyama grama	4	3	2	4	3	4	2
Gandhara grama	3	2	4	3	3	3	4

From the above chart it may be seen that there is no fundamental difierence between the sruti relations of the svaras of the sadja and madhyama grama, as the fixed tonic i.e. Sa is placed on the 4th sruti in each case, the only difference being on the relative sruti positions of pancama and dhaivata. But in the case of Gandhara grama, the fixed tonic has shifted its position, thereby changing the entire pattern in the sruti relation. Nishada has taken one sruti from sadja, another from dhaivata. Similarly gandhara has taken one sruti from rishava, another from madhyama. Even Bharata did not discuss gandhara grama ; it was mentioned by Narada, but he did only refer to the grama as existing in the 'Svargaloka'.

The explanation given by Sarangadeva, as also the comments made by Dr. Kunhan Raja about the names of these three gramas according to the sadja, gandhara and madhyama notes is far from satisfactory. 'Sadja is the principal, since it is the first [svara], similarly because it has more ministers'. That explains, according to Sarangadeva, why sadja grama has been so named. But if sadja has more ministers (it has two, in Ma and

Pa, ministers meaning concordant samvadı notes) than those of the other notes in the sadja grama, madhyama and gandhara should also have more ministers than those of the other notes in the Ma-grama and Ga-grama respectively.

The following chart shows the vadi-samvadi relations in the three gramas, the 2nd, 3rd and 4th columns indicating samvadi notes in the respective gramas (accepting the principle that the distance between the vadi and samvadi would be 8 and 12 srutis apart) :

Vadi note	Sa-grama	Ma-grama	Ga-grama
S	M, P	M	M
R	D	P, D	D
G	N	N	D, N
M	S	S, N	S
P	S	R	R, G
D	R	R	R, G
N	G	G, M	G

The chart shows that Sa has two ministers in Ma and Pa in the sadja grama and no other note has the same advantage. But in the Ma-grama as well as in Ga-grama, the position is entirely different. It is true that Ma has two ministers, in Sa and Ni, in the Ma-grama, but other two notes, R and N have also two ministers each, in P, D and G, M respectively. Similarly G has two ministers, in D and N, in the Ga-grama, but D has also two ministers, in R and G. So, the argument of the author as well as of the translator that 'it (Sa) has more ministers than the others' does not hold good, at least, in the cases of Ma-grama and Ga-grama.

The only valid explanation possibly lies in the fact that Sa is the first note in the first murchana in Sa-gramā, Ma is also the first note in the first murchana in Ma-grama. It may be assumed that Ga is also the first note in the first murchana in the Ga-grama. No reference has been made of the Ga-grama murchana in the Sangitratnakara, as evinced from the following sloka :

Murchanetyucyatey gramadvayey tah sapta sapta ca

[These (Murchana) are seven in each of the two gramas]. These two gramas do not obviously include Gandhara grama. The music pattern in ancient times was mostly governed by the arrangement of murchana and so it occupied a very important position in determining the nature of music. It is quite probable that the importance of the sadja and madhyama notes in the first murchanas in the Sa-grama and Ma-grama and of the gandhara note in the first murchana of Ga-grama respectively prompted some of the musicologists to name the gramas accordingly.

Seasonal time has been ascribed for singing in these three gramas, the sadja, madhyama and gandhara grama, during hemanta (the season prior to the winter), grishma (hot) and varsha (rainy). Sarangadeva then describes murchana in the following sloka :

Kramatsvaranang saptanamarohascabarohanam

[The recitation in the ascending and in the descending order of the seven svaras is called Murchana].

These seven murchanas in the two gramas are arranged as follows :

Starting note	Sadja grama	Starting note	Madhyama-grama
1. Sa (Madhya-sthana)	Uttarama-ndra	Ma (Madhya-sthana	Sauviri
2. Ni (Mand-rasthana	Rajani	Ga (,,)	Harinasva
3. Dha (,,)	Uttarayata	Ri (,,)	Kalopanata
4. Pa (,,)	Suddhasadja	Sa (,,)	Suddhamadhya
5. Ma (,,)	Matsarakrita	Ni (Mandra-sthana)	Margi
6. Ga (,,)	Asvakranta	Dha (,,)	Pauravi
7. Ri (,,)	Abhirudgata	Pa (,,)	Hrishyaka

The seven svaras are to be recited in succession in both ascending and descending orders as SRGMPDN (SNDPMGR) or MPDNSRG (MGRSNDP). These svaras may be extended from one sthana to the other. This may be seen in item 2 of col. 2 of the above chart where the Rajani murchana is stated ; the murchana being N (mandrasthana) or again in the Margi murchana in the madhyama grama. In fact, murchanas in items 1 and 2 to 7 in sadjagrama and those in item 1-4 and 5-7 in the madhyama grama are extended into two sthanas.

These fourteen murchanas are all with suddha notes, but if kakali and antara svaras are taken then there would be fifty-six varieties as follows :

14 varieties with suddha svaras in the two gramas
14 ,, ,, kakali nishada ,, ,, ,, ,,
14 ,, ,, antara gandhara ,, ,, ,,
14 ,, ,, kakali nishada & antara gandhara

Each of these murchanas have seven orders, beginning from S (and continuing with NDPMGR) as the first note. Dr. Kunhan Raja has explained these orders in his translation-work (p. 72-73). These orders in which the svaras are arranged are called Kramas. For theoretical considerations the number of total Kramas are 56 (murchanas) x 7 = 392 Kramas, Krama meaning order in succession.

Sarangadeva next discusses a very important topic i.e. tana. So far it may be understood from the following sloka :

Tanah syumurchanah suddah shadabaurubitikritah

[The tanas are Suddha Murchanas converted into shadavas and auduvas].

That there is no basic difference between a murchana and tana has been accepted, rather it may be said that the tanas are born out of the murchanas. Murchana uses all the seven notes, while tana uses five or six notes. In modern practice, a tana may comprise any number. The translator of Sangitratnakara further elaborates the issue. If in a suddha murchana, only six svaras or if only five svaras are taken up, it is called a suddha tana [the text must be taken to mean that a suddha tana is a suddha murchana]. It may rather be said that a murchana is complete when it uses all the notes in succession. If it does not use all the notes, we have the incomplete murchana, or no murchana at all, which may be termed as tana. The translator gives the following details regarding tanas :

"In the two (gramas), these are accepted as the forty-nine shadava (Tanas).

In the shadja grama there are separately twenty-one audava tanas."

Murchanas, both complete and incomplete, having the svaras sung without any definite order become 'Kutatanas'. A Murchana is complete when all the seven svaras are taken up at the same time......If the svaras are sung only in the ascending order, we have suddha tanas. If they are sung in all possible combinations with no order, we get kuta tanas.

Asampurnasca sampurna byutkramoccaritasvarah
murchanah kutatanah syustatsankhyamavidadhmahey

The next important point that Sarangadeva describes is the particular *prastara* which he terms as *Khandameru*. Here is quoted the full English version of the slokas :

"From the second half of stanza 63 to the first half of stanza 66, what is called *Khandameru* is described. This is a graph to determine the form of svara combination for a particular number in the series and for determining the number in the series for a particular svara combination given. These two processes are respectively called nashta and uddishta......uddishta is the finding out the number of the tana of given form...nashta is the method of determining the form of a tana when the number is given." C. Kunhan Raja has tried to elaborate these methods with specific examples in his translation work.

There is little discourse on 'sadharana' where four distinct kinds are mentioned as Kakali, Antara, Sadja and Madhyama. As specific example, an instance is cited :

"Sa has normally the first four srutis. If the first is taken up by Ni and the fourth by Ri, it is sadja sadharana."

The tenth sloka in sub-chapter 5 is very important. Here Sarangadeva refers to the term Raga in connection with Jati sadharana. The translator puts the corresponding sloka as per :

"That singing which is common among Jatis derived from the same Grama and having the same Amsa, noble people speak of a Jati sadharana. Some people speak of this Jati sadharana as Ragas. The frequent svara in a Jati is equivalent to the vadi svara of a Raga."

In the next sub-chapter, the musicologist describes varna and alamkara. Varna, which is of four kinds, is the pada in a gradual process of singing and are as follows : Sthayi, Arohi, Avarohi and Sancari. Sancari is, by far, the most difficult as well as ornamental in having the first three varnas mixed up together. In modern terms these are Sthayi, Antara, Sancari and Abhog, Sancari coming third in the sequence. Then begins the descriptions, with specific examples, of the alamkaras which are sixty-three in number and divided among the varnas as : Sthayi varna 7, Arohi varna 12, Avarohi varna 12, Sancari varna 25 and other Alamkaras 7.

Sthayi varna : Prasannadi, Prasannanta, Prasannadyanta, Prasannamadhya, Kramarecita, Prastara, Prasada (7)

Arohi varna : Vistirna, Niskarsha, Vindu, Abhyuchhaya, Hasita, Prenkshita, Akshipta, Sandhiprachhadana, Udgita, Udbahita, Tribarna, Veni (12)

Abarohi varna : the twelve alamkars as those of arohi varna in the descending order (12)

Sancari varna : Mandradi, Mandramadhya, Mandranta, Prastara, Prasara, Vyabritta, Skhalita, Parivarta (ka), Akshepa, Vindu, Udbahita, Urmi, Sama, Prenksha, Niskujita, Shyena, Krama, Udghattita, Ranjita, Sannibrittaprabritti (ka), Venu, Lalitasvara, Hunkara, Hladamana, Abalokita (25)

Another Seven : Taramandraprasanna, Mandrataraprasanna, Abartaka, Sampradana, Vidhuta, Upalolaka (lola ?), Ullasita.

The alamkaras are also described by Bharata in details with specific notes as Prasannadi (SSS′) Prasannanta (S′S′S) Prasannadyanta (SS′S) Prasannamadhya (S′SS′) It would seem from the series, that the alamkara evokes the prasanna rasa which is symbolised in the base sadja note. (S′ meaning tara Sa)

The seventh sub-chapter is devoted to the description and illustration of Jati (this has been described earlier in this treatise in a summary form). There are seven pure Jatis as Sadji, Arshavi, Gandhari, Madhyama, Pancami, Dhaivati and Naishadi, meaning that each Jati has for its principal pattern, one particular note. There are ten characteristics of a Jati described earlier. There are three more characteristics as Antaramargi, Alpatva and Bahutva. There are another eleven separate varieties which spring up from combination of the modifications. These were also discussed in the chapter on Natyasastra. Sarangadeva might have taken this aspect exclusively from Bharata's work.

Svaraprastara : The most important point of raga development is the method known as svaraprastara. This may be achieved by applying the algebric formula ${}^{n}P_{r}$ i.e. finding the permutation of n things taking r numbers at a time. We can, therefore, find easily the numerical figure obtained this way :

1.	Taking one note at a time out of 7 notes :	$^{7}P_{1} =$	7
2.	Taking two notes at a time (,,) :	$^{7}P_{2} =$	42
3.	Taking three ,, at a time (,,) :	$^{7}P_{3} =$	210
4.	Taking four ,, at a time (,,) :	$^{7}P_{4} =$	840
5.	Taking five ,, at a time (,,) :	$^{7}P_{5} =$	2520
6.	Taking six ,, at a time (,,) :	$^{7}P_{6} =$	5040
7.	Taking seven ,, at a time (,,) :	$^{7}P_{7} =$	5040
	Grand total		13699

[$^{7}p_{6}$ and $^{7}p_{7}$ have the same mathematical values, as factorial zero is equal to one.]

Let us take concretely one example, say, taking two notes at a time of n things i.e. 7 things, ${}^{7}P_{2}$:

(a) Regular order ; SR SG SM SP SD SN
Reverse order : RS GS MS PS DS NS
(b) Eliminating S, RG RM RP RD RN/GR MR PR DR NR
(c) Eliminating R, GM GP GD GN/MG PG DG NG
(d) Eliminating G, MP MD MN/PM DM NM.
(e) Eliminating M, PD PN/DP NP. & P, DN/ND Total : 42

Besides the Svaragatadhyaya, the three other chapters that seem to be important from the music-aspects, are the Ragvivekadhyaya, Prakirnadhyaya and Prabandhyadhyaya. These three chapters deal successively the raga-system, the different lakshmanas of the musicians and of music demonstration, and the types of geetis prevalent till his time.

The Ragadhyaya (we shall refer to Ragvivekadhyaya simply as Ragadhyaya for the sake of convenience) deal systematically with five types of geetis, seven suddha ragas, five vinna ragas, three goura ragas, eight besara ragas, seven sadharana ragas, eight uparagas, twenty ragas, and lastly, Sarangadeva refers to the musicologist Jashtika who has described fifteen Bhashajanakaragas.

In the second sloka of the Ragadhyaya Sarangadeva states :

Pancadha gramaraga syuh pancageetisamasrayat ;
geetayah panca suddha ca bhinna gouri ca besara.
sadharanageeti suddha syadbakrairlalitaih svaraih
bhinna bakraih svaraih sukshmairmadhurairgamakai
rjukta

The grama ragas [Ragas were generally termed as grama ragas at that time] were sung and developed through the five geetis as suddha, vinna, gouri, besara and sadharani. Besara seems to be an abbreviation of Begasvara that Sarangadeva refers to later in the sixth sloka of the chapter. The different characteristics of the geetis were also enumerated. Steadiness (notes in order) and beauty i.e. qualities of abakra and lalita svaras, are the characteristics of suddha geeti ; where the notes do not follow the order [bakra as SRMG instead of SRGM], but used in a sweet and delicate manner with application of gamak as SSM, RRP the geetis are called vinna (bakra, sukshma and madhura svaras with gamaks). Gouri is the third type which encompasses the three gamuts as mandra, madhya and tara (saptaks) ; notes are used here more hurriedly, but there is a depth in tonal quality. Besara or Begasvara is sung in a complete cycle beginning from sthayi, proceeding along arohi and abarohi varnas, culminating in the sancari. It should have the requisite colour (raktijukta) and have an emotive design. The fifth type is the sadharani, a composite pattern developed out of the four geetis described above.

Sarangadeva then describes the gramaragas in detail. The thirty gramaragas belong to five geetis as suddha containing seven grama ragas, vinna five, gauri three, besara eight and sadharani seven. Out of these thirty gramaragas a few are known and sung still today (notes have, however, been altered) as Pancam, Malabakaisik (Malkosh ?), Hindol and Kukuv (a variety of Bilawal).

There are eight uparagas. The author has just mentioned the names, but the term uparaga has not been defined properly, nor its connection with the gramaragas are clear from the commentaries. The names of the uparagas as Sakatilaka to Nagapancama are obsolete now.

Ragas are twenty in number of which Sree, Nat (Natta), Bhairab, Megh, Kamod, Natanarayan (Nattanarayana) are known even today.

The subdivisions as bhasha, bibhasha and antarabhasha have been derived from fifteen ragas (gramaragas, meaning hereby parent ragas). There are ninety-six bhasha ragas, twenty bibhasha ragas and four antarabhasha ragas totalling a number of one hundred and twenty such subdivisions.[7]

Ninety-six bhasharagas are broadly divided in four categories according to their distinctive types. They have been termed as

Mukhya, Svarakhya, Desakhya and Uparagaja. Matanga has described these categories as Samkirna, Deshaja, Mula and Chayamatra. It seems that Mula, Chayamatra and Samkirna correspond to modern raga categories as Shuddha, Shalaga (Chayalaga) and Samkirna.

All the ragas belonging to the various categories mentioned earlier were termed by some musicologists as Marga ragas, but through successive centuries these have undergone continuous fusion and changes according to contemporary taste as well as to distinctive style of rendering in various schooling. At a later date these ragas came to be known as Deshi ragas and were divided in four broad classes as

1. Raganga 2. Bhashanga 3. Kriyanga 4. Upanga

Owing to the long tradition these ragas were grouped as Purvaprasiddha and Adhunaprasiddha meaning thereby ancient and modern types. So we get four broad divisions of Purvaprasiddha ragas and four of Adhunaprasiddha ragas in Raganga, Bhashanga, Kriyanga and Upanga types.

1. Purbaprasiddha Raganga contains eight ragas of which Sankarabharan and Dipaka are still known.

2. Purbaprasiddha Bhashanga contains eleven ragas of which Chaya is known and sung even today.

3. Purbaprasiddha Kriyanga contains twelve raga names each of which is followed by the letter 'kri' ; the ragas were demonstrated on some social occasion. A few such names are Bhabakri, Sivakri etc.

4. Purvaprasiddha Upanga contains three ragas as Purnati, Debal and Gurunjika, all unknown today.

Similarly, fifty-two Adhunaprasiddha ragas have been classified as under :

1. Adhunaprasiddha Raganga contains thirteen ragas of which Madhyamadi (Madhumadhabi Sarang ?) Todi, Bangal (Bhairab), Gurjari (Gurjari Todi ?) Basantaka (Basanta ?), Dhannyasi (Dhanesri ?), Deshi, Desakhya (or Debsakh ?) are known and sung.

2. Adhunaprasiddha Bhashanga contains nine ragas of which Sabari, Belabali, Nagaddhvani and Natta are more or less known (Sabari is, however, unknown).

3. Adhunaprasiddha Kriyanga contains three ragas of which Ramakriti (Ramakri or Ramkeli ?) is quite popular even today.

4. Adhunaprasiddha Upanga contains twenty-seven ragas of which Chaya-Belabali, Bhairabi, Chhayanatta, Mallari, Gour Mallar have come to stay.

Thus the total list of ragas, adding all the varieties together as under Gramaraga (30) Uparaga (8) Raga (20) Bhasha (96) Bibhasha (20) Antarbhasha (4) Purbaprasiddha Raganga etc. (34) and Adhunaprasiddha Raganga etc. (52), comes to a total of 264.

The most interesting study of the ragas during the entire period relates to the continuous fusion and mixture at various levels. This fusion took place in a number of ways. It may be seen that Jati ragas were first created out of the predominance of a certain definite svara. From the suddha jatis there evolved vikrita jatis by the fusion of two, three, four and even five predominant svaras. The next stage of development saw the particular traditional culture of a place and its localised music pattern getting mixed up with the vikrita jatis. The folk tunes were no less responsible also for the creation of later ragas[8].

During the centuries, the jatiragas and gramaragas underwent constant and continuous change and fusion resulting thereby the broad and clear classification as Deshi sangita—which was sung according to certain fixed tonal pattern, and termed as 'Raga' at a later date.

Sarangadeva then goes on to give details of the *ragalapa* of each individual raga and its characteristic features as origin, graha, amsa, nyasa, character, rasa and so on. We may take, for example, tha bhasha raga Malabakaisik. The details are given as :

Malabakaisik Bhasha (Malkosh ?)

1. Graha : Madhyam
2. Amsa : Madhyam
3. Nyasa : Sadja
4. Bhasha : Bangal
5. Jati : Sampurna and so on.

It may be seen that the present form of the raga Malkosh has retained the first three characteristics faithfully. It has now been transformed into an oudava raga, with five notes as S g M d n, (small letters = komal notes) from its ancient pattern of sampurna jati with all the seven notes. In this way the author gives relevant details of the ragas as well as their svaraprastara.

The third chapter has been named by Sarangadeva as Prakirnakadhyaya. From the very second sloka he has described the qualities of the Baggeyakar :

Bang maturucyatey geyang dhaturityabhidhiyatey
bacang geyang ca kurutey jah sa baggeyakarakah

The composition is called the *matu*, the music form its *dhatu*. One who can convincingly bring to light both the lyrical composition as well as the music form is known as baggeyakar. In modern times the music form is composed of the four varnas as sthayi, antara, sancari and abhog. With sufficient control over the use and delivery of svaras, the baggeyakar should also have the proper sense of laya, tala and control over the varieties of rhythmic patterns. He should understand and apply correctly the predominant rasa in between and be conversant with the artistic device all through. He should also have a good knowledge of 'deshi sangita'. His voice should move easily the three saptaks, with gamak wherever necessary, that qualifies the term 'hridyasarira', lastly he should be able to perform *alapti* with skill and grace.

Sarangadeva next describes the qualities of a musician :

Hridyasabdah susariro grahamokshabicakshanah
ragaraganga bhashanga kriyangopangakobidah

... ...

suddhachayalagabhigga sarbakakubiseshabit
.....sarbadoshabibarjitah

A musician should be thoroughly conversant with the raga, raganga, bhashanga, kriyanga and upanga types, be expert in demonstrating prabandha ganas, should know the proper alapa and must have control over laya and tala and be flawless.

There are, according to the author, four categories of musicans as grouped under

1. Baggeyakar (Musician-cum-scholar)
2. Gayaka (Musician or artiste)
3. Sikshaka (Teacher)
4. Rasika (Connoisseur)

The musicians again form three broad divisions among themselves as

1. Artiste, who performs as a solo musician (ekala)
2. Artistes who perform in duet singing (jamala)
3. Artistes who perform in chorus singing (brindagayana)

The author then specifically points out twentyfive bad qualities for a musician. Unwanted mannerism, unnecessary loud voice, swift bodily movements, lack of proper artistic sense, nasal voice are only a few that are mentioned here.

Sound is the basis of all music, so the author has described the different characteristics that embody human voice-reproductions. Normally, there are four such types as

1. Khahul 2. Narat 3. Bombak 4. Misraka

Caturbhedobhabechchabdah khahulo naratabidhah
bombako misrakasceti tallakshmanamathocyatey

The most important portion of the Prakirnadhyaya seems to be the Ragalapti. Alapti is that portion of the song which reflects the character and basic design of a raga and expresses faithfully its inner emotions and feelings. Alapti is of two kinds : ragalapti and rupakalapti. Ragalapti embodies the main notes in a successive order and emphasizes the proper positions of the relevant notes. Rupakalapti is connected with the prabandha geeti, sung in a definite raga and tala and exposes the geeti in all its forms, shape and colour. The definite stages of the geeti should be sung in a systematic manner from the beginning to the end. It brings out not only the latent emotiveness, but the actual tinge of the raga proper while delineating the geeti.

Rupakalapti is again divided into two parts, pratigrahanika and bhanjani. In the first part, the different 'sthayas' are demonstrated. The alapa, in all its parts, is to be demonstrated in the following manner :

Rupakasthena ragena talena ca bidhiyatey
ja prokta rupakalapti sa punardvibidha bhabet

The raga will emerge from the four definite positions ; the next stage elaborates the various 'sthaya'. The structure of the composition of a raga and its establishment as a physical reality may be termed as 'sthayas'. The sthaya is of two kinds, asamkirna and samkirna. Sarangadeva has elaborately dealt with the asmkirna and samkirna sthayas which are innumerable in number. The elaboration of the sthaya would centre round the main note (vadi or amsa svara). The raga would then come to stay and the listener would feel that the raga has now been established. In the ultimate stage, the total outline of the song would reach a climax only to depict the 'tirobhava' (the end along the descending order) at the culminating stage. In modern practice, 'abhog' symbolizes the concluding stage of a song proper.

The alapti portion, though treated only in a few slokas, is important from the practical aspect of music as a whole. Even a musicologist of contemporary times would feel that the procedure as laid down by Sarangadeva and practised by the musicians of the past, has had its long-drawn tradition, spread over down the centuries, so as to unite the hoary ancients with the moderns.

The Prabandhyadhya forms the most important and exhaustive chapter and the author has elaborately dealt with the various divisions and subdivisions of the prabandhageeti while emphasizing their individual traits and characteristics.

The adhyaya opens with the sloka :

Ranjakah svarasandarbho geetamityabhidhiyatey
gandharba ganamityasya vedyayamuditam

and not only the prabandhageetis are composed of 'ranjaka svara-sandharava', meaning combination of various sweet notes, but this form is sung by the 'anadisampradaya'. Sarangadeva has not defined the term, but both Simhabhupala and Kallinatha have offered their views to give us reasonable explanation of the word. Kallinatha has stated that the songs, sung by the sect as 'anadi', actually takes us to a very long and old tradition ; in fact, from time immemorial and handed down to contemporary musicians by the gandharvas.

The author next goes on to the classification of the 'geeta', that are broadly divided into two categories as nibaddha and anibaddha. The nibaddha geeti, as against the anibaddha, has three broad divisions as prabandha, bastu and rupaka. The author first attempts at defining the prabandha geeti that forms the major part.

In the fifth sloka of the adhyaya he clearly defines that dhatu and anga bind the geetis and that is why the prabandha is so termed as being bound in a fixed and definite manner by its parts as dhatus and angas.

Prakristarupey bandhah iti prabandhah

The prabandha geetis have four dhatus as described in slokas 7 and 8 as udgraha, melapaka, dhruba and abhog, correspon-ding to the modern terminology as sthayi, antara, sancari and abhog. The word 'dhruba' that means fixed and steady would never be discontinued by the singer. There is also the portion 'antara' between dhruba and abhog, though it is not specifically mentioned in the text. The six parts of the prabandhageeti (anga) are svara, biruda, pada, tenaka, pata and tala. These signify the various parts of the geeti proper corresponding to the various limbs of the human body.

Prabandhoangani shat tasya svarasca birudang padam
tenakah patatalau ca prabandhapurushasya tey

As per distribution of these angas the prabandha geeti is again classified into five broad divisions according to jatis ; these are medini (with 6 angas), nandini (5) dipani (4), bhabani (3) and tarabali (2). The colloqual terminology corresponding to these five jatis are sruti, niti, sena, kabita and campu.

Svara means notes as sadja, rishava, gandhara etc. and biruda are complementary qualities symbolizing 'bols' of the drums and their qualitative effects. Pada means the entire composition, tenaka signifies the aesthetic qualities while pata and tala determines the *bol* and rhythmic pattern.

As music itself is divided into two broad divisions as nibaddha and anibaddha, prabandha geeti is also classified into two broad categories as nirjukta and anirjukta. The detailed classification may be given a shape as under :

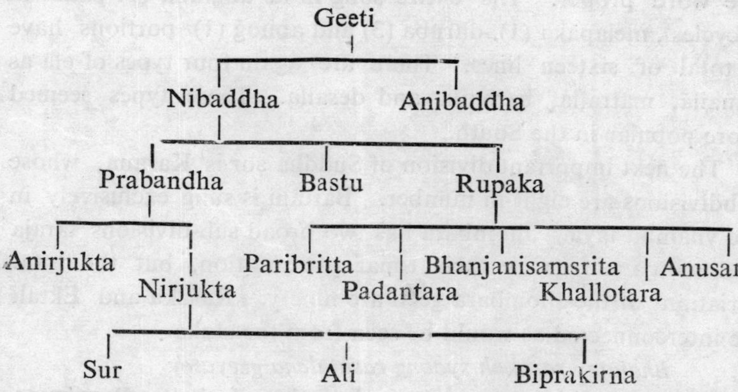

The above chart shows how elaborate the geeti structure prevailed in Hindu music. This also clarifies the highly imaginative and scrutinizing vision of the composers, their concept of raga structure and their control over rhythmic variations and so on. The author has dealt exhaustively only with the prabandhageeti and its varieties. He has just mentioned bastu, but has not described it, while he added only a few slokas for his analysis of rupaka out of a total of 380 slokas in the Prabandhadhya. Sarangadeva has described Suddha sura which are eight in number of which Ela, Karan, Bartani, Jhombara, Rasaka and Ektali form the most important types from the historical aspect. Ela songs begin either with the *atita* or the *anaghata* tala, it is composed in bisama chhanda. This forms the common characteristic of the Ela types. We might compare old Bengali tappas sung in the madhyaman tala wherein the first line is generally sung in bisama or sama chhanda having its 'som' either in the *atita* or *anaghata*. Mantha and pratitala are its accompanying talas. The emotive contents are heroism, sacrifice, patience etc. Sarangadeva has elaborately dealt with the singing process of the ela geeti. The author has also conceived an underlying philosophy describing the form, the image of Lord Visnu. Kamadeva and the Goddess Laxmi are symbolized in the letters composing the word proper. The entire song in its udgraha (11 padas in 3 cycles), melapaka (1), dhruba (3) and abhog (1) portions have a total of sixteen lines. There are again four types of ela as ganaila, matraila, barnaila and desaila. These types seemed more popular in the South.

The next important division of Suddha sur is Karana, whose subdivisions are eight in number. Bartani is sung exclusively in the vilambit laya. Jhombara has two broad sub-divisions taraja and ataraja as regards their tonal presentation, but the total variations of the Jhombara geeti are ninety. Rasaka and Ektali are interconnected as would be seen from the sloka :

Bhajatey rasakah syoang rasatalena geeyatey

Kallinatha, in his commentary, has described the Rasaka as belonging to the tarabali jati.

The Ali varieties of the prabandha geeti has twentyfour varieties of which Kaibara (Karapata ?), Totaka, Ragakadambaka, and Panchatalesvara are important. Kaibara is of special importance because of its traditional association with the development of Kheyal. Sarangadeva has described kaibara as :

Patai syatang dhrubodgrahau Kaibarey nyasanang grahey
sarthakairarthahinaisca pataih sa dvibidho matah

The kaibara variety is conceived by the patas which compose udgraha and dhruba, and the song is terminated at the udgraha, meaning thereby that the udgraha is sung again before its conclusion. Matanga has also referred to this form in his Brihaddesi and described that Kaibata (kaibara) is sung in the marga tala along with patakshara (bol patterns of the percussion instruments).

Among the Biprakirna variety under the prabandha type of geeti there are a great number, of which thirty-six categories are mentioned in the music texts. Of these again we get a few which have direct bearing with the succeeding music-types. These are Tripadi, Cachari, Caryya and Mangal. Caryya and Mangal deserve our special attention specially with the music-culture traits of Bengal. Caryya geeti forms by itself the earliest examples of Bengali poetry, while mangalageetis compose the most humane utterances during the middle ages before and after Sree Chaitanya's advent. Sarangadeva was of the opinion that the caryyageeti was prevalent in other parts of India too. The caryyas are composed in paddhari (sanskrit : pajhjhatika) chanda and are divided into purna and apurna as per rhythmic variations. The singing style has again been differentiated because of its character being split into samadhruba and bisamadhruba. The description of caryya is as follows :

Paddhariprabhitichandah padanuprasasobhita

It is, however, debatable whether the mangalgeeti as prevalent in the eastern parts of Bengal has any connection with mangala variety of the prabandhageeti within the biprakirna type. But the author has pointed out that the mangala geeti is sung only in the Kaisiki and Botta ragas ; and further, there is the rhythm as the mangala chanda.

Sarangadeva has lastly described Shalagasur i.e. chayalaga. This is quite important as some musicologists have had the impression that the modern dhrupada has its connection with the shalaga-sur dhruba-prabandha. By the word chayalaga we mean those type of songs wherein traces of suddha geetis are found. Jati, kapal, kambal, gramaraga, uparaga, bhasa, bibhasha and antarabhasa from the suddha geetis. Those songs that have not followed strictly the above suddha geetis have been termed chayalaga or shalaga-sur. In modern times chayalaga ragas are much in practice as Suddhakalyan having traces of Bhupali, or Hambir having traces of Kedar and so on. The seven type of geetis that are incorporated within the shalaga-sur group are dhruba, mantha, pratimantha, nissaruka, addatala, rasa and ektali.

Next comes Rupaka that is described as

Gunanvitang doshahinang nabang rupakamuttamam
ragena dhatumatubhyang tatha talalaurubauh ;
nutanai rupakang nutnang ragah sthayantarairnabah.
dhatu ragansabhedena matostu nal ata bhavet ;
... ...
layagrahabiseshena talanang nabata mata ;
... ...
cahandoganagrahanyasa prabandhabayabairnabaih
oudubaparaparyaya racana nabatang brajet.

The above slokas are self-explanatory so far the description of Rupaka is concerned. In its raga design, during the sthayi portion, in its dhatu and matu one might feel a sense of novelty ; the very structure of the nibaddhageeti is shaped here in a new design. There are perhaps fusion of ragas, the laya has its variety and the talas are new most of the time. This imaginative flair and the attempt at innovation, both in structure and tonal design, make the Rupaka a distinct pattern by itself ; it is not, therefore, improbable that the origin of kheyal has its source not only in kaibaras, but also in the rupaka type.

The ancient Hindu music culminates with the prabandha and rupaka songs which give us, on the protracted plane, the rudiments of dhrupad and kheyal that were later to dominate the music horizon of the mediaeval and modern era ; and along with these music forms, the concept of raga also becomes universal in Indian music.

---

1. The name of the commentaries are Kalanidhi and Sudhakara respectively by Kallinatha and Simhabhupala.

2. Other two reliable commentaries are by Kesava in Sanskrit and Gangarama in Hindi.

3. The date about Locana Kavi has, however, remained controversial. Dr. Sukumar Sen fixed his date at a much later period.

4. Sanyal Amiyanath : Prachin Bharatey Sangitcinta

5. ibid

6. Such reference may be found in most of the ancient texts ; and names of birds and animals have now become a part of legend having association of their vocal notes with those of standard musical notes.

7. Svami Prajnanananda has added a chapter on 'Evolution of Ragas' in his book 'Historical Development of Indian Music'. He has given therein a total of four charts which help in classifying the raga divisions and sub-divisions.

Rajyesvar Mitra, in his treatise 'Sangit Samiksha', has clearly stated that bhasha is connoted as a type of alapa of a particular grama raga. From this pattern has evolved bibhasha and antarabhasha.

8. Ratanjankar, S. N: Loukik O Ragsangiter Utsasandhaney.

Slokas in the text

Creative Awakening :

p.6 Om tat sabiturbarenyam

श्रों तत् सबितुर्वरेण्यं

In Retrospect

p.9 Nṛtyagītavāditrabacha

नृत्यगीतवादित्रबच्च

Sāmavedey sahasraṅ gītyupāyah

सामबेदे सहस्रं गीत्युपायः

etairbbābaistu gāyanti sarbah śākhāh pṛthak-pṛthak

एतैर्भाबैस्तु गायन्ति सर्वः शाखाः पृथक्-पृथक् ।

p.10 hṛdyūrdhanāḍīsaṅlagnā

हृदूर्धनाड़ीसंलग्ना

Transformations

Stage i : pre-Vedic Period

p.12 Ṣaḍjey badati mayūro gābho rambhanti carṣavah
aja badati gāndhāro krouñcanādaṣna madhyamey
puṣpasādhāraney kāley kokilah pañcamey svarey
aśvastu dhaivatey prāha kunjarastu niṣādabān

षड़्जे वदति मयूरो गाभो रम्भन्ति चार्षभः ।

श्रज वदति गान्धारो क्रौञ्चनादष्ण मध्यमे ॥

पुष्पसाधारणे काले कोकिलः पञ्चमे स्वरे
अश्वस्तु धैवते प्राह कुञ्जरस्तु निषादवान् ॥

Stage ii : Vedic Period

p.21 Om bhūrbhubah svhah

ओं भूर्भुवः स्वः

Stage iii : Vedic notes and later forms

p.28 Gāndharvaṅ janmayā proktaṅ svaratālapadātmakam
Padam tasya vabedbastu svaratālānubhāvakam

गान्धर्वं यन्मया प्रोक्तं स्वरतालपदात्मकम् ।
पदम् तस्य भवेदवस्तु स्वरतालानुभावकम् ॥

p.29 Chandagānagrahanyasah prabandhābayabairnabaih

छन्दगानग्रहन्यासः प्रवन्वावयवैर्नवैः

The Epics and Haribaṃsa

p.36, Jātivih saptavirjuktam tantrīlayasamanvitam
rasaih śṛṅgārakaruṇahāsyaraudrabhayānakaih
birādibhi rasairjuktaṅ kāvyametadgāyatām

जातिभिः सप्तभिर्युक्तं तन्त्रीलयसमन्वितम्
रसैः श्रृंगारकरुणहास्यरौद्रभयानकैः
वीरादिभिः रसैर्युक्तं काव्यमेतद्गायताम् ॥

p.37 dibasey biṅsati sargā geyā

दिवसे विंशति सर्गा गेया

gāyatāṇ madhuraṅg geyaṅ tantrīlayasamanvitam

गायतां मधुरं गेयं तन्त्रीलयसमन्वितम्

Vipancī nabtantrīkā

विपञ्ची नवतन्त्रीका

ebaṅ bahubidho jneyah śabda ākāśasambhavah

एवं वहुविधो ज्ञेयः शव्द आकाशसम्भवः

Musicologists before and after Bharata

p.42 Sankhabherīmṛdaṅgapaṇavatūṇavavīṇaballakī
.........snigdhamadhuramanojna
svaravenunināditanirghoṣarutena bodhisattvam

शंखभेरीमृदंगपणवतूणववीणावल्लकी

·····. ··स्निग्धमधुरमनोज्ञ

स्वरवेनुनिनादितनिर्घोषरुतेन वोधिसत्त्वम् ॥

Saharṣya-ṛṣava-gāndhāra-dhaivata-niṣāda-madhyama kaiśikī

सहर्ष्य-ऋषभ-गान्धार–धैवत-निषाद-मध्यम कैषिको

p.45 tantrīrādyā nayanasalilaih sāraitvā kathaṅcit
bhūoh bhūah svayamadhikritāṅ mūrchanānāṅ bismaranti

तन्त्रीराद्यानयनसलिलैः सारयित्वा कथंचित् ।

भूयोः भूयः स्वयमधिकृतां मूर्च्छनानां विस्मरन्ति ॥

p.46 mūrchanāparigṛhītakaiśikaih
kinnarairuṣasī gītamangalah

मृच्छ्‌र्नापरिगृहोतकैशिकैः

किन्नरैरुषसी गीतमंगलः ॥

prayoganipuṇaih prajoktṛibhih

प्रयोगनिपुणैः प्रयोक्तृभिः

The Puranas

p.50 Jachrutva Raibatah kā'ān muhūrtamiba manyatey

यच्छ्रुत्वा रैवतः कालान मुहूर्तमिव मन्यते

p.53 Ṣaḍjacatuśrutirgeyārṣavastriśruti smritā
dviśrutiṣcāpi gāndhāro madhyamasca catuśruti
catuśruti pañcama syāt triśrutidhaivata tathā
dviśrutistu naiṣādasyat ṣadjagrāmey svarāntarey

षड्जचतुश्रुतिर्ज्ञेया ऋषभस्त्रिश्रुति स्मृता ।
द्विश्रुतिश्चापि गान्धारो मध्यमश्च चतुश्रुति ॥
चतुश्रुति पञ्चम स्यात त्रिश्रुतिधैवत तथा ।
द्विश्रुतिस्तु नैषादस्यात पड्जग्रामे स्वरान्तरे ॥

p.55 Grāmadvayajjāyata iti jātaya

ग्रामद्वयज्जायत इति जातय

p.56 daśabidham jātilakṣmanam

दशविधम् जातिलक्ष्मनम्

Grahāmśau tāramandrau ca nyāsāpanyāsa eba ca
alpatvam ca bahutvam ca ṣāḍavauḍuvite tathā

ग्रहांशौ तारमन्द्रौ च न्यासापन्यास एव च ।
अल्पत्वम् च वहुत्वम् च षाड़वौड़ुविते तथा ॥

p.57 ārohī cabārohī ca sthaīsañcārinau tathā

आरोही चावरोही च स्थायीसञ्चारीनौ तथा

Nāradīyaśikṣā : A prelude to Nāṭyaśāstra

p.65 Nāṭyaśāstrasya dvitīyabhāgasya ṣaṭṣu adhyāeṣu kebalaṅ gītavādyam ālocitam. Nāradīyaśikṣāṅ bihāya etadeva hi sangītaśāstrabiṣayam prācīnatamamālocitam.

नाट्यशास्त्रस्य द्वितीयभागस्य षटषु अध्यायेषु केवलम् गीतवाद्यम् आलोचितम्। नारदीयशिक्षां विहाय एतदेव हि संगीतशास्त्रविषयम् प्राचीनतममालोचितम्।

Ātmā bibakṣamānoyaṅ manah prerayatey manah
dehasthaṅ bahnimāhanti sa prerayati mārutam.

आत्मा विवक्षमानोयं मनः प्रेरयते मनः
देहस्थं वह्निमाहन्ति स प्रेरयति मारुतम्।

p.66 manah kāyāgnimāhanti sa prerayati mārutam

मनः कायाग्निमाहन्ति स प्रेरयति मारुतम्।

p.67 Prathamaśca dvitīyaśca tritīyotha caturthakah
mandra kruṣṭo atisvāra etān kurbanti sāmagāh

प्रथमश्च द्वितीयश्च तृतीयोथ चतुर्थकः।
मन्द्र क्रुष्टो अतिस्वार एतान् कुर्वन्ति सामगाः॥

tānarāgasvaragrāmamūrchanānaṇ

तानरागस्वरग्राममूर्च्छनानां

Saptasvarastrayogrāmamūrchnāstekabiṅśati
tānā ekonapancāśadityetat svaramandalam

सप्तस्वरस्त्रयीग्राममूर्च्छनास्तेकविंशति।
ताना एकोनपञ्चाशदित्येतत् स्वरमंडलम्॥

p.68 Bhūrlokajjāyatey ṣadjo bhubarlokacca madhyamah

भूर्लोकज्जायते षड्जो वर्लोकत्र मध्यमः।

Gānasya tu daśabidha gunabṛttistadjathā
raktaṅ purna malaṅkṛtaṅ prasannaṅ byaktaṅ bikruṣtaṅ
Ślakṣnaṅ samaṅ sukumāraṅ madhura miti guṇah

गानस्य तु दशविध गुणवृत्तिस्तदयथा
रक्त पूर्णमलंकृतं प्रसन्नं व्यक्तं विक्रुष्टं
श्लक्ष्णं समं सुकुमारं मधुरमिति गुणः ॥

p.69 dhaivatah kampita jatra

धेवतः कम्पित यत्

Jah sāmagānāṅ prathamah sa benormadhyamah svarah
Jo dvitīya sa gāndhārastritīyastṛṣavah smṛtah
caturthah ṣaḍja ityāhu pañcama dhaivato bhavet
ṣaṣtho niṣādo bijñeya saptamah pañcamah smritah

यः सामगानां प्रथमः स वेनोर्मध्यमः स्वरः ।
यो द्वितीय स गान्धारस्तृतीयस्तृषभः स्मृतः ॥
चतुर्थः षड्ज इत्याहु पञ्चम धैवतो भवेत् ।
षष्ठो निषादो विज्ञेय सप्तमः पञ्चमः स्मृतः ॥

p.70 ṣaḍjasambādinī kekā

षड्जसंवादिनी केका

Jathāpsu caratāṅ mārgo mīnanaṅ nopalabhyatey
ākāśey bihangānaṅ tatbatsvaragatā śrutih
Jathā dadhani sarpih syāt kaṣthastho bā jathānaley
prajatney nopalabhyatey tatbatsvaragatā srutih

यथाप्सु चरतां मार्गो मीनानां नोपलभ्यते ।
आकाशे विहगांनां तत्वतस्वरगता श्रुतिः ॥
यथा दधनि सर्पि स्यात् काष्ठस्थो वा यथानले ।
प्रयत्ने नोपलभ्यते तत्वतस्वरगता श्रुतिः ॥

The Nāṭyaśāstra

p.71 prayogastribidho jhyeṣāng bijjnayo nāṭakāsraya

प्रयोगस्तृविधी ह्येषां विज्ञयो नाटकाशृय

ḍhruvābidhāney kartabyā jātiganā (projoktṛvih)

ध्रुवाविधाने कर्तव्या जातिगाना (प्रयोक्तृभिः)

p.72 Kutapabinyāsa

कुतपविन्यास

Jattu tantṛkṛtaṅ proktaṅ nānātodyasamāśrayam
gāndharvamiti tajgeyaṅ svaratālapadāśrayam

यत्तु तन्त्रीकृतं प्रोक्तम् नानातोद्यसमाश्रयम् ।
गान्धर्वमिति तज्गेयं स्वरतालपदाश्रयम् ॥

p.73 madhyamagrāmey tu śrutyapakṛṣtah pañcama kāryyah

मध्यमग्रामे तु श्रुत्यपकृष्टः पञ्चम कार्यः

p.74 asāṅ ṣaḍjaniṣāda dhaivatapañcamamadhyama gāndhārarṣabha
adyā svarā ṣadjagrāmey

आसां षड्जनिषाद धैवतपञ्चममध्यम गान्धारऋषभ
आद्या स्वरा षड्जग्रामे

āsāṅ madhyamagāndhārarṣabhaṣaḍjaniṣādadhaivata
pañcama anupūrbādyāh svarāh madhyamagrāmey

आसां मध्यमगान्धारऋषभषड्जनिषादधैवत पञ्चम
आनुपूर्वाद्याः स्वराः मध्यमग्रामे

mūrchanāsaṅśṛtāstānāścaturāṣīti

मूर्च्छनासंश्रितास्तानाश्चतुराशीति

kramajuktā

क्रमयुक्ता

p.75 Jātayo dvibidhā suddhā bikṛtāśca
parasparāṅ sanjogādekādaśa nirbartayanti

जातयो द्विविधा शुद्धा विकृताश्च ।
परस्परां संयोगादेकादश निर्वतयन्ति ।।

gāndhārīṣaḍjābhyāṅ saṅsargajjāyate candhrī

गान्धारीषड़्जाभ्यां संसर्गज्जायते चान्ध्री

p.77 Daśabidham jātilakṣmanam
grahāṅśau tāramandrau ca nyāsāpanyāsa eba ca
alpatvaṅ ca bahūtvaṅ ca ṣāḍavauḍubitey tathā

दशविधम् जातिलक्ष्मनम्
ग्रहांशौ तारमन्द्रौ च न्यासापन्यास एव च
अल्पत्वं च वहुत्वं च षाड़वौड़्विते तथा ।।

p.78 ebameto budhairjneyā jātayo daśālakṣmaṇah
svaih svaiśca karaṇairjojya padesvabhinayairapi

एवमेतो वुधैर्ज्ञेया जातयो दशलक्षणः
स्वैः स्वैश्च करणैर्योज्या पदेश्वभिनयैरपि ।।

p.79 Hāsya śṛngārayoh kāryau svarau madhyamapañcama
ṣaḍjarṣavau ca kartabyau bīraraudradbhuteṣvathā
gāndharaśca niṣādaśca kartabau karuṇey rasey
dhaivataśca prajuktabyo bībhatsey sa bhayānakey

हास्य श्रृंगारयोः कार्यौ स्वरौ मध्यमपञ्चम ।
षड़्जऋषभौ च कर्तव्यौ वीरारौद्राद्भुतेस्वथा ।।
गान्धारश्च निषादश्च कर्तवौ करुणे रसे ।
धैवतश्च प्रयुक्तव्यो वीभत्से स भयानके ।।

Ṣaḍjodicyabatī caiba ṣadjamadhyā tathaiba ca
madhyamapañcama bāhulyat kārjyaṅ śṛngārahāsyayoh

षड़्जोदिच्यवती चैव षड़्जमध्या तथैव च ।
मध्यमपञ्चम वाहुल्यात् कार्य्यं श्रृंगारहास्ययोः ।।

p.80. etān samāsṛtān samyaglamkārannibodhata

एतान समाश्रितान् सम्यग्लंकारन्निबोधत

p.81. Śaśinā birahiteba niśā bijaleba nadī latā bipuṣpeba abibhūṣiteba ca strī gītiralamkārahīnā syāt

शशिना विरहितेब निशा विजलेव नदी लता विपुष्वेव
अविभुषितेव च स्त्री गीतिरलंकारहीना स्यात् ॥

Prathamā māgadhī jneyā dvitīyā tvardhamāgadhī sambhavitā tṛtīyā ca caturthī pṛthulā smṛtā

प्रथमा मागधी ज्ञेया द्वितीया त्वर्द्ध मागधो ।
सम्भाविता तृतीया च चतुर्थी पृथुला स्मृता ॥

p.82. dhruvājogan binaiba hi

ध्रुवायोगं विनैव हि

Gāndharva eba jojyastu nityan gānaprojoktṛvih

गान्धर्व एव यीज्यस्तु नित्यं गानप्रयोक्तृभिः ।

Tisro gatibṛttayah pradhānyena grāhya citrabṛttidakṣiṇāsceti. Tāsān vādyatālalayagītimārgapradhānyāni jathāsvāng vyāñjanāni bhabanti.

तिस्रो गतिवृत्तयः प्राधान्येन ग्राह्य चित्रवृत्तिदक्षिणाश्चेति । तासां वाद्यताललयगीतिमार्गप्राधान्यानि यथास्वां व्याञ्जनानि भवन्ति ।

p.83. Saptatantrī bhavetcitrā bipañcī nabatantrīkā bipañcī konavādyā syātcitrā cāngulibādanā

सप्ततन्त्री भवेच्चित्रा विपञ्ची नवतन्त्रीका ।
विपञ्ची कोनवाद्या स्याच्चित्रा चंागुलिवादना ॥

Jastu talaṅ na jānati na sa gātā na bādakāh

यस्तु तालं न जानाति न स गाता न वादकाः ।

Chandyokṣarapadānāṅ hi samatvaṅ jat prakīrtitam
kalākalāntarakṛtaḥ sa layo mānasanggitah.

छन्द्योक्षरपदानां हि समत्वं यत्प्रकीर्तितम्
कलाकालान्तरकृतः स लयो मानसंज्ञितः ॥

p.85. Vākyavarṇā jhyālamkārā layā jātyatha pāṇayah
dhruvamanyonyasambandhā jasmāntasmād dhruvā smṛtā.

वाक्यवर्णाह्यालंकारा लया यात्यथ पाणयः
ध्रुवमन्योन्यसम्बन्धा यस्मान्तस्माद ध्रुवा स्मृता ॥

p.86 Jati (h) sthanaṅ prakāraśca pramānaṅ nāma caiba hi

जाति (ः) स्थानं प्रकारश्च प्रमाणं नाम चैव हि

p.88 Purṇasvaraṅ vādyabicitravarṇaṅ
tṛsthānasovaṅ tṛjata tṛmātram
raktaṅ samaṅ ślakṣnamalamkṛtaṅ ca
sukhaprajuktaṅ madhuraṅ ca gānam

पूर्णस्वरं वाद्यविचित्रवर्णं
त्रिस्थानशोभं त्रियतं त्रिमात्रम् ।
रक्तं समं श्लक्ष्णमलंकृतं च
सुखप्रपुक्तं मधुरं च गानम् ॥

p.89 Jyeṣhthamadhyakaṇistthaṅ tu patrānāmabadhārya ca
gambhīraṅ madhuraṅ hṛdyamājagāmāśramaṅ tatah

ज्येष्ठमध्यकणिष्ठं तु पत्रानामवधार्य च
गम्भीरं मधुरं हृद्यमाजगामाश्रमं ततः ॥

p.92 Mayūrī madhyamey grāmey ṣadjey tvardhā tathaiba ca
karmāravī tu gāndhārey sādhāranasamāśrayah

मायूरी मध्यमे ग्रामे षड्‌जे त्वर्धा तथैव च ।
कर्मारवी तु गान्धारे साधारणसमाश्रयः ।।

p.92 gītavādyakalālayagrahamokṣabiśāradotha laghuhastah
citrapāṇirbidhijna siddhisthāney dhruvākuśalah
kalābhiratah madhurahastah sunibiṣto raktamārjano-
balabān
subihitośarīrabuddhih sańsiddho vādakah śreṣtthah

गीतवाद्यकलालयग्रहमोक्षविशारदोऽथ लघुहस्तः ।
चित्रपाणिविधिज्ञ सिद्धिस्थाने ध्रुवाकुशलः ।।
कलाभिरतः मधुरहस्तः सुनिविष्टो रक्तमार्जनोवलवान् ।
सुविहितशरीरबुद्धिः संसिद्धो वादकः श्रेष्ठः ।।

p,93 Vādye ca gītey ca suprajuktey
nāṭyaprayogey na bipattimeti.

वाद्ये च गीते च सुप्रयुक्ते
नाट्यप्रयोगे न विपत्तिमेति ।।

Bṛhaddeśī

p.94 Deśey deśey prabṛttasau dhvanirdeśīti sanggītah

देशे देशे प्रवृत्तऽसौ ध्वनिर्देशीति संज्ञितः ।

Tato bindustaṭo nadastato mātrāstvanukramāt
varṇastu mātrākodbhūtā

ततो विन्दुस्ततो नादस्ततो मात्रास्त्वनुक्रमात्
वर्णास्तु मात्राकोद्भूता ... ...

p.95 Dhanirjonih parā jneyā dhavnih sarbasya Kāraṇam
ākrāntaṅ dhvaninā sarbaṅ jagat sthābarajangamam

ध्वनिर्योनिः परा ज्ञेया ध्वनिः सर्वस्य कारणम्
आक्रान्तं ध्वनिना सर्वं जगत् स्थावरजंगमम् ॥

Dhvanistu dvibidhah prokto vyaktāvyaktabibhāgatah

ध्वनिस्तु द्विविधः प्रोक्तो व्याक्ताव्यक्तविभागतः ।

Gīyatey sānurāgena

गीयते सानुरागेन

Na nāden bina gītaṅ na nāden bina svarāh

न नादेन विना गीतं न नादेन विना स्वराः

Nādarūpaih smṛto Brahmā nādarūpo Janārdana
nādarūpā parā saktirnādarūpo Mahesvarah.

नादरूपैः स्म्रतो व्रह्मा नादरूपो जनार्दन ।
नादरूपा परा शक्तिर्नादरूपो महेश्वरः ॥

Tanmaddhye saṅsthitah prāṇah prāṇād bahnisamu-
dbhavah
bahnimārutasanjogānnādah samupajāyatey

तन्मध्ये संस्थितः प्राणः प्राणाद् वह्निसमुद्भवः
वह्निमारुतसंयोगान्नादः समुपजायते ॥

p.96 Sūkṣmaścaibātisūkṣmaśca vyāktoavyaktaśca kṛttṛmah
सूक्ष्मश्चैवातिसूक्ष्मश्च व्याक्तोऽव्यक्तश्च कृत्रिमः ।

Śruyanta iti śrutayah

श्रुयन्त इति श्रुतयः

Sopānapadakramenā

सोपानपदक्रमेन

p.97 Svayaṅ jo rājatey jasmāt tasmādeṣa svara smṛtah

स्वयं यो राजते यस्मात् तस्मादेष स्वरः स्म्रतः

Rāgajana (ko) dhvanih svara iti

रागजन (को) ध्वनिः स्वर इति

Nityoabinaśī. Vyapakah sarbagatah

नित्योऽविनाशी । व्यापकः सर्वगतः

Rāgasya rāgatvaṅ janayati

रागस्य रागत्वं जनयति

p.98 Samūhabācinau grāmau svaraśrutyādisanjutau
jathā kuṭumbinah sarba ekībhutvā basanti hi

समूहवाचिनौ ग्रामौ स्वरश्रुत्यादिसंयुतौ
यथा कुटुम्विनः सर्व एकीभूत्वा वसन्ति हि ॥

Svaraśrutimūrchanātanājātirāgaṇaṅ vyabasthāpanatvaṅ nāma prayojanaṃ

स्वरश्रुतिमूर्च्छनातानाजातिरागानां व्यावस्थापनत्वं नाम प्रयोजनम्

p.99 Mūrchatey (?) jena rāgo hi mūrchanetyabhisanggita

मूर्च्छते (?) येन रागो हि मूर्च्छनेत्यभिसंज्ञित

Nanu mūrchanātānayo ko bhedah. Ucyatey......
mūrchanārohakrameṇa tānoabarohakrameṇa bhavatīti bhedah.

ननु मूर्च्छनातानयो को भेदः। उच्यते। ...... मूर्च्छनारोहक्रमेण तानोऽवरोहक्रमेण भवतीति भेदः।

Dvibidhā tānakriyā tantryā prabeśānāṅ nigrahastatha

द्विविधा तानक्रिया तन्त्र्या प्रबेशानां निग्रहस्तथा।

p.100 Jasmādjjāyatey rasapratītirārabhyata iti jā (jatah ?) tayah

यस्माज्जायते रसप्रतीतिरारभ्यत इति या (यतः ?) तयः

Jasminnaṅsey kṛyamāney rāgābhivyakti (bhih ?) rbhabati syoaṃśa

यस्मिन्नंशे क्रियमाने रागाभिव्यक्ति (भिः) र्भवति स्योऽशं।

Ranjako janacittānāṅ sa ca rāga udahṛtah

रञ्जको जनचित्तानां स च राग उदाहृतः

ṣadjāṅśau pañcamo nyāsa kaiśikījātisambhavah
tathākarmārabhījāteh svaraih pūrṇaiśca kaiśikah.

षड्जांशौ पञ्चमो न्यास कैशिकोजातिसम्भवः।
तथाकर्मारभीजातेः स्वरैः पूर्णैश्च कैशिकः॥

Sangītratnākara

p.104 Gītena prīyate deva......

Sāmagītirato Brahmā vīṇāasaktā Sarasvatī
kimanye jakṣagandharvadevadānavamānavāh

... ...

dharmārthakāmamokṣānāmidamebaikasādhanaṃ

गीतेन प्रीयते देव .....

सामगीतिरतो ब्रह्मा वीणाऽऽसक्ता सरस्वती

किमन्ये यक्षगन्धर्वदेवदानवमानवाः

... ...

धर्मार्थ काममोक्षानामिदमेवैकसाधनम् ॥

Veenābādanatatvaggah śrutijātibiśāradah

tālaggaścaprayāsena mokṣamargaṅ sa gachati

वीणावादनतत्त्वज्ञः श्रुतिजातिविशारदः ।

तालज्ञश्चाप्रयासेन मोक्षमार्गं स गच्छति ॥ (याज्ञबल्क्य)

Brahmagranthijamārutanugatinā cittena hritpankajey

sūrīṇāmanuranjaka śrutipadaṅ joayaṅ svayaṅ rājatey

jasmād grāmabibhāgavarṇaracanāalaṃkārajātikṛamo

bande nādatanu tamuddhurajagadgītaṅ mudey

Śankaram

ब्रह्मग्रन्थिजमारुतानुगतिना चित्तेन हृत्पंकजे

सूरीणामनुरंजक श्रुतिपदं योऽयं स्वयं राजते ॥

यस्माद् ग्रामविभागवर्णरचनाऽलंकारजातिक्रमो

वन्दे नादतनुं तमुद्धुरजगदगीतं मुदे शंकरम् ॥

p.105 Gītaṅ vādyaṅ tathā nṛttaṅ trayaṅ sangītamucyatey

गीतं वाद्यं तथा नृत्तं त्रयं संगीतमुच्यते

Mārgo deśīti tad dvedhā tatra mārgah sa ucyatey

jo mārgito birincādaih prajukto Bharatādivih

debasya purato śambohrniyatābhyudayapradah

deśey deśey janānaṅ jaducyā hṛdayaranjakaṃ
gītaṅ ca bādanaṅ nṛttaṅ taddeśītyabhidīyaṭey

मार्गो देशीति तद् द्वेधा तत्र मार्गो स उच्यते
ये मार्गितो विरिञ्चादैः प्रयुक्तो भरतादिभिः
देवस्य पुरतो शम्भोर्नियताभ्युदयप्रदः
देशे देशे जनानां यदुच्या ह्लदयरंजकम्
गीतं च वादनं नृत्तं तद्देशीत्यभिदीयते

p.106 Deśey deśey prabṛttasau dhvanirdeśīti sanggitah
देशे देशे प्रब्रत्तऽसौ ध्वनिर्देशीति संज्ञितः

p.107 Nirbikāraṅ nirākāraṅ sarveśvaramanaśvaram
sarvaśakti ca sarbaggaṅ tadaṅśa jībasanggakah
निर्विकारं निराकारं सर्वेश्वरमनश्वरम्
सर्वशक्ति च सर्वज्ञं तदंश जीवसंज्ञकः
Asti kuṇḍalīni brahmaśaktirādhārapankajey
अस्ति कुण्डलीनि व्रह्मशक्तिराधारपंकजे

p.108 Jatah prāṇāgnisanjogāttena
यतः प्राणाग्निसंयोगात्तेन
Bahnimārutasanjogānnadaḥ samupajāyate
वह्निमारुतसंयोगान्नादः समुपजायते
Pancasthānasthita kramāt
पंचस्थानस्थित क्रमात्

p.109 śrabaṇāchhrutayo
श्रवणाच्छ्रुतयो

Uchochataratājuktā

उच्चोच्चतरतायुक्ता

...jaḥ snigdho anuraṇanātmaka
svato ranjayati śrotṛicittaṅ sa svara ucyatey

···यः स्निग्धोऽनुरणनात्मक

स्वतो रञ्जयति श्रोतृचित्तं स स्वर उच्यते

śrabaṇendriyagrājhyatvād dhvanireba śrutirbhavet

श्रवणेन्द्रियग्राह्यत्वाद ध्वनिरेव श्रुतिर्भवेत्

p.110 Anantyaṅ hi śrutināṅ ca sūcayanti bipaścita
jathā dhvanibiśeṣānāmanantyaṅ gaganodarey
uttālapabanodbelajalarāśisamudbhava
iattāṅ pratipadyantey na tarangaparamparā

अनन्त्यं हि श्रुतिनां च सूचयन्ति विपश्चित

यथा ध्वनिविशेषानामनन्त्यं गगनोदरे ॥

उत्तालपवनोद्वेलजलराशिसमुद्भव

इयत्तां प्रतिपद्यन्ते न तरंगपरम्परा ॥ (कोहल)

Dīptā āyatā ca karunā mṛdurmadhyetijātaya

दीप्ता आयता च करुणा मृदुर्मध्येतिजातय

p.112 Cyuto actyuto dvidha saḍjo dviśrutirvikṛto bhavet
sādhāraṇey kākalitvey niṣādasya ca dṛśyatey

च्युतोऽच्युतो द्विधा षड्जो द्विश्रुतिर्विकृतो भवेत्

साधारणे काकलित्वे निषादस्य च दृश्यते ॥

p.113 Śrutidvayaṅ cyetṣadjasya niṣāda saṅśrayettadā
sa kākali madhyamaśca gāndhārastvantara svaraḥ

श्रुतिद्वयं च्येतषड्जस्य निषाद संश्रयेत्तदा

स काकलि मध्यमश्च गान्धारस्त्वन्तर स्वरः ॥

Caturvidhā svarā vādī samvādī ca vivādyapi
anuvādī ca vādī tu prayogey bahulah svaraḥ
śrutayo dvādaśāṣtau ba jajorantaragocharaḥ
mitha saṅvādīnau tau

चतुर्विधा स्वरा वादी संवादी च विवाद्यपि
अनुवादी च वादी तु प्रयोगे वहुलः स्वरः ॥
श्रुतयो द्वादशाष्टौ वा ययोरन्तरगोचरः
मिथ संवादोनौ तौ ॥

p.114 Sārī bīrey adbhutey raudrey dhī bibhatsey bhayānakey
kārjau gāni tu hāsyaśṛngārayormapau

सारी वीरेऽद्भुते रौद्रे धो वीभत्से भयानके
कार्यौ गनि तु हास्यश्रृंगारयोर्मपौ ॥

p.115 Grāma svarasamūhah syānmūrchanādeh samāśrayaḥ
tau dvau dharātaley tatra syātṣadjagrāma ādimaḥ
dvitīya madhyamagrāmah

ग्राम स्वरसमूहः स्यान्मूर्च्छनादेः समाश्रयः
तौ द्वौ धरातले तत्र स्यात्षड्जग्राम आदिमः ॥
द्वितीय मध्यमग्रामः

Jatha lokey janasamūho grāma ityucyatey, ebamātra svarasamūho grāma iti bibakṣitah.

यथा लोके जनसमूहो ग्राम इत्युच्यते एवमात्र स्वरसमूहो इति विवक्षितः ॥

śvarānaṅ mūrchanātānajātijātyaṅ śakātmanām
byābasthitaśrutinaṅ hi samūho grāma īṣyatey

स्वरानां मूर्च्छनातानाजातिजात्यं शकात्मनाम्
व्यावस्थितश्रुतिनां हि समूहो ग्राम ईष्यते ॥

p.117 Mūrchanetyucyatey gr**ā**madvayey tāh sapta sapta ca

मूर्च्छनेत्युच्यते ग्रामद्वये तः सप्त सप्त च

p.118 Kramatsvar**ā**n**ā**ṅ sapt**ā**n**ā**m**ā**rohaścabarohaṇam

क्रमात्स्वरानां सप्तानामारोहश्चवरोहणम्

p.119 T**ā**n**ā**h syūmūrchan**ā**ḥ suddh**ā**ḥ ṣādavauḍubitikṛtaḥ

तानाः स्यूमूर्च्छनाः शुद्धाः षाड़वौड़ुवितिकृतः

p.120 Asampūrnaśca sampūrna byutkramoccāritasvaraḥ
mūrchanāh kūṭat**ā**n**ā**h syustatsankhy**ā**m**ā**vidadhmahey

असम्पूर्णश्च सम्पूर्ण व्युत्क्रमोच्चारितस्वरः
मूर्च्छनाः कुढ तानाः स्युस्ततसंख्यामाविदधमहे ।।

p.123 Pañcadhā grāmar**ā**gā syuh pañcagītisamāsrayt**ā**
gītayah pañca suddh**ā** ca bhinn**ā** gouri ca besar**ā**
sādh**ā**ranagīti suddh**ā** syādbakrairlalitaih svaraih
bhinnā bakraiḥ svaraiḥ sūkṣmairmadhurairgama-
kairjukt**ā**

पञ्चधा ग्रामरागा स्यु पञ्चगीतिसमाश्रयात्
गीतयः षञ्च शुद्धा च भिन्ना गौरी च वेसरा ।
साधारणगीति शुद्धा स्याद्वक्रैर्ललितैः स्वरैः
भिन्ना वक्रैः स्वरैः सूक्ष्मैर्मधुरैर्गमकैर्युक्ता ।।

p.127 Bāṅ maturucyatey geyaṅ dhaturityabhidhiyatey
bācaṅ geyaṅ ca kurutey jaḥ sa bāggeyakārakaḥ

वां मातुरुच्यते गेयं धातुरित्यभिधीयते
वाचं गेयं च कुरुते यः स वाग्गेयकारकः ।।

Hṛdyaśabdah suśariro grahamokṣabicakṣaṇah
rāgarāgānga bhāṣānga kṛyāngopāngakobidah
... ...
suddhachāyālagabhigga sarbakākubiśeṣabit
...sarbadoṣabibarjitaḥ
ह्ययशव्द सुशरीरो ग्रहमोक्षविचक्षरणः
रागरागागं माषागं क्रियागोंपागंकोविदः
... ...
शुद्धच्छायालगभिज्ञ सर्वकाकुविशेषवित्
...सर्वदौषविवर्जितः ।।

p.128 Caturbhedobhavechabdah khāhulo nāraṭābhidhah
bombako miśrakāśceti tallakṣmanamathocyatey.
चतुर्भेदोभवेच्छव्द खाहुलो नारढाभिदः
वोम्वको मिश्रकाश्चेति ताह्लक्ष्मरणमथोच्यते ।।

p.129 Rūpokasthena rāgena tālena ca bidhiyatey
ja prokta rupakālapti sa punardvibidhā bhabet
रूपकस्थेन रागेन तालेन च विधोयते ।
य प्रोक्त रूपकालप्ति स पुनर्द्विविधा भवेत् ।।

p.130 Ranjakoh svarasandarbho gītamityabhidhīyatey
gāndharba gānamityasya bhedaaymudīritaṃ
रञ्जकः स्वरसन्दर्भो गीतमित्यभिधोयते ।
गान्धर्व गानमित्यस्य भेदऽयमुदोरितम् ।।

prakṛṣtarūpey bandhah iti prabandhah
प्रकृष्ठरूपे वन्धः इति प्रवन्धः

p.131 Prabandhoangaṇi ṣaṭ tasya svaraśca birudaṅ padaṃ
tenakah pāṭatalau ca prabandhapuruṣasya tey

प्रवन्धोऽगांनि षट तस्य स्वरश्च विरुदं पदम् ।
तेनकः पाटतालौ च प्रवन्धपुरुषस्य ते ॥

p.132 bhajatey rasakaḥ syoaṅ rasatālena gīyatey
भजते रासकः सोऽयं रासतालेन गीयते

p.133 Pāṭai syātaṅ dhrubodgrahau kaibarey nyāsanaṅ grahey
sārthakairarthahīnaiśca pāṭaih sa dvibidhomataḥ
पाठै स्यातां ध्रुवोद्ग्राहौ कैवाढे न्यासनं ग्रहे ।
सार्थकैरर्थहीनैश्च पाटैः स द्विविधो मतः ॥

paddharīprabhṛtichhandāh pādānuprasaśobhitā
पद्धड़ीप्रभृतिच्छन्दाः पादानुप्रासशोभिता

p.134 Guṇānvitaṇ doṣahīnaṅ nabaṅ rūpakamuttamam
rāgena dhātumātubhyaṅ tatha tālalayauḍubauh
nūtanai rūpakaṅ nūtnaṅ rāgah sthāyāntarairṇabah
dhātu rāgaṅśabhedena matosta nabatā bhabet

... ...

layagrahabiśeṣeṇa tālānāṅ nabatā matā

chandogāṇagrahanyāsaprabandhābayabairnabaih
ouḍubāparaparjaya racana nabatan brajet.

गुणान्वितं दोषहीनं नवं रूपकमुत्तमम् ।
रागेन धातुमातुभ्यां तथाताललयौड़ुवौः ॥

नूतनं रूपकं नूत्नं रागः स्थायान्तरैर्नवः ।
धातु रागांशभेदेन मातोस्तु नवता भवेत् ॥

... ...

लयग्रहविशेषेण तालानां नवता मता ।

... ...

छन्दोगणग्रहन्यासप्रबन्धावयवैर्नवैः ।
औडुवापरपर्याया रचना नवतां व्रजेत् ॥

Select Bibliography

English

Annals of the Bhandarkar Oriental Research Institute

Bell, Clive : Art

Bhatkhande, B. N : A Short Historical Survey of the Music of Upper India.

A Comparative Study of some of the Leading Music Systems of the 15th, 16th 17th & 18th Centuries

Bhattacharya, Arun : Dimensions

Bosanquet, B : History of Aesthetics

Butcher, S. H. : Aristotle's Theory of Poetry and Fine Arts.

Croce, B. : Aesthetic

Cultural Heritage of India (The) : (Vol. I, Vol. II, Vol. III, Vol. IV. Introduction by Dr. S. Radhakrishnan, Dr. C. P. Ramaswami Aiyar, Dr. S. N. Dasgupta and Shri Bhagawan Das.)

Danielou, Alain : Introduction to the Study of Musical Scales

Day, C. R : The Music and Musical Instrument of Southern India and Deccan

Fyzee-Rahaman, Atiya Begum : The Music of India

Fox-Strangways, A. H. The Music of Hindostan

Gangooly, O. C. : Ragas and Raginis

Ghosh Manomohan : The Natyasasrta (Tr.)

Goswami, O. : The Story of Indian Music

Hanslick, Edward : The Beautiful in Music

Helmoltz, Hermann L. F. : On the Sensations of Tone

Jeans, Sir James : Science and Music

Jones, Sir William ; On the Musical Modes of the Hindus

Langer, Susanne K. : Philosophy in a New Key

Meyer, Leonard B : Emotion and Meaning in Music

Popley, Rev. H. A. : The Music of India

Prajnanananda, Svami : A History of Indian Music
Historical Development of Indian Music

Raja, C. Kunhan : Sangitratnakara (Tr.)

Richards, I. A. : Principles of Literary Criticism

Sambomoorthy, P : History of Indian Music

Seashore, Carl E. : Psychology of Music

Sachs, Curt : The Rise of Music in the Ancient World, East and West

Tagore, Sir S. M. : Six Principal Ragas
Universal History of Music

Willard, Captain A. N. : A Treatise on Indian Music (Music of Hindostan)

Wilson, Anne C. : A Short Account of the Hindu System of Music

Bengali

গঙ্গোপাধ্যায়, অর্ধেন্দ্রকুমার : রাগরাগিণীর নামরহস্য

গুপ্ত, অতুলচন্দ্র : কাব্যজিজ্ঞাসা

গোস্বামী, ক্ষেত্রমোহন : সঙ্গীতসার

চৌধুরী প্রমথ ও চৌধুরানী ইন্দিরা দেবী : হিন্দু সংগীত

দাশগুপ্ত সুরেন্দ্রনাথ : সৌন্দর্যতত্ত্ব

ঠাকুর অবনীন্দ্রনাথ : বাগিশ্বরী শিল্প প্রবন্ধাবলী

ঠাকুর রবীন্দ্রনাথ : সংগীতচিন্তা

প্রজ্ঞানানন্দ, স্বামী : সংগীত ও সংস্কৃতি
ভারতীয় সংগীতের ইতিহাস

বন্দ্যোপাধ্যায়, কৃষ্ণধন : গীতসূত্রসার

ভট্টাচার্য, অরুণ : রবীন্দ্রসংগীতে স্বর সংগতি ও সুরবৈচিত্র্য
সংগীতচিন্তা

ভট্টাচার্য, আশুতোষ : বঙ্গীয় লোকসংগীত-রত্নাকর

ভট্টাচার্য, সাধনকুমার : ক্রোচের এস্থেটিক ও এসেন্স অব এস্থেটিক

মিত্র রাজ্যেশ্বর : সংগীতসমীক্ষা
: বাংলার সংগীত

রতনজংকার, শ্রীকৃষ্ণনারায়ণ : লৌকিক ও রাগসংগীতের উৎসসন্ধানে

রায়, নীহাররঞ্জন : বাঙ্গালীর ইতিহাস

রায়চৌধুরী, বিমলাকান্ত : ভারতীয় সঙ্গীতকোষ

রায়চৌধুরী, বীরেন্দ্রকিশোর : হিন্দুস্থানী সঙ্গীতে তানসেনের স্থান
সঙ্গীতবিজ্ঞান প্রবেশিকা

সান্যাল, অমিয়নাথ : প্রাচীন ভারতের সংগীতচিন্তা

সান্যাল, অযোধ্যানাথ : বৈদিক স্বররহস্য

সেন, রাধামোহন : সঙ্গীততরঙ্গ

Sanskrit

कल्लिनाथ : संगीतरत्नाकर (टीका)

कालिदास : ग्रन्थावली

जयदेव : गीतगोविन्दम्

नारदी (य) शिक्षा

भरत मुनि : नाट्यशास्त्र

मतंग : बृहद्देशी

शार्ङ्गदेव : संगीतरत्नाकर

सिंहभूपाल : संगीतरत्नाकर (टीका)

INDEX